PRAISE FOR *UNCLUTTER YOUR SOUL*

"Written through the perceptive eyes of a stylist, *Unclutter Your Soul* approaches soul care with a fresh, welcoming, and applicable slant. You'll want to read, gift, and highlight this gem of a book over and over again."

—MYQUILLYN SMITH, *NEW YORK TIMES*
BESTSELLING AUTHOR, *WELCOME HOME*

"In a society of chaos and overwhelm, Trina has done the heavy lifting of exposing the root and offers us courage and strength to overcome. I've watched her live this message up close, and I can't be more thrilled this powerful resource is in your hands. This is a must-read for our cultural moment!"

—REBEKAH LYONS, BESTSELLING AUTHOR,
RHYTHMS OF RENEWAL AND *YOU ARE FREE*

"It is one thing to fill our lives with beauty, and it is another thing to disabuse our lives of what's broken. This process of decluttering our inner home, as Trina puts it, requires courage, personal responsibility, and a vision for living more spaciously and soulfully. If you have added all the right things to your life and you still find yourself stuck, read these words. Trina will lead you lovingly toward letting go."

—LEEANA TANKERSLEY, AUTHOR, *HOPE ANYWAY*

"Practical and poetic, Trina McNeilly offers readers everything they need for their soul journey. Seamlessly blending personal storytelling, biblical knowledge, and modern psychology, Trina has created a guide that is as beautifully written as it is helpful. For all of us with anxious hearts and monkey minds, Trina will become your most trusted soul sister."

—KATHY IZARD, AUTHOR, *THE LAST ORDINARY HOUR*

"Once I began reading *Unclutter Your Soul*, it quickly became the friend I couldn't wait to return to. With the grace and compassion of your most trusted companion, Trina invites us to consider the living home within each of us and offers blueprints that create space for more peace and joy. This breathtaking book provides a guide we all need to do the difficult but worthy work of acknowledging the clutter that impedes health and wholeness, creating space for truth to take root, and finding the courage to walk in a new way. The words on these pages will leave you comforted, challenged, and changed. Of that I have no doubt."

—NICOLE ZASOWSKI, MARRIAGE AND FAMILY THERAPIST AND
AUTHOR, *FROM LOST TO FOUND* AND *WHAT IF IT'S WONDERFUL?*

"If you've ever cleared out your closet with the secret hope that the space and order you create will bring the calm and peace the deepest parts of you long for, this book is for you. *Unclutter Your Soul* isn't a temporary quick fix to brighten your day but a lasting gift to bring light and space to your inner world. It's a gift you'll never regret giving yourself.
"Going before us with generosity and understanding, Trina shares a roadmap to unclutter the basements, attics, and closets of our souls that we keep hidden or don't know are hurting. By showing us how to clear out these tenderest of places, she gifts us the way to the lasting freedom and joy we crave."

—NIKI HARDY, AUTHOR, *BREATHE AGAIN: HOW
TO LIVE WELL WHEN LIFE FALLS APART*

"Can we *really* breathe deeper and walk lighter and overcome those things that clutter our "inner home" and rob us of peace? Through compelling personal stories and biblical promises, Trina demonstrates the answer is undoubtedly *yes!* Come along to discover the wide-open, spacious inner-life you long for."

—JEANNIE CUNNION, AUTHOR, *DON'T MISS OUT*

Un-
clutter
Your
Soul

Un-clutter Your Soul

OVERCOME WHAT OVERWHELMS YOU

Trina McNeilly

W PUBLISHING GROUP

AN IMPRINT OF THOMAS NELSON

Published in Nashville, Tennessee, by W Publishing Group, an imprint of Thomas Nelson.

Author is represented by the Christopher Ferebee Agency, www.christopherferebee.com

Thomas Nelson titles may be purchased in bulk for educational, business, fund-raising, or sales promotional use. For information, please email SpecialMarkets@ThomasNelson.com.

Unless otherwise noted, Scripture quotations are taken from THE MESSAGE. © 1993, 2002, 2018 by Eugene H. Peterson. Used by permission of NavPress. All rights reserved. Represented by Tyndale House Publishers, a Division of Tyndale House Ministries.

Scripture quotations marked AMP are taken from the Amplified® Bible (AMP). © 2015 by The Lockman Foundation. Used by permission. www.Lockman.org. Scripture quotations marked AMPC are taken from the Amplified® Bible (AMPC). © 1954, 1958, 1962, 1964, 1965, 1987 by The Lockman Foundation. Used by permission. www.Lockman.org. Scripture quotations marked ESV are taken from the ESV® Bible (The Holy Bible, English Standard Version®). © 2001 by Crossway, a publishing ministry of Good News Publishers. Used by permission. All rights reserved. Scripture quotations marked KJV are taken from the King James Version. Public domain. Scripture quotations marked NIV are taken from the Holy Bible, New International Version®, NIV®. © 1973, 1978, 1984, 2011 by Biblica, Inc.™ Used by permission of Zondervan. All rights reserved worldwide. Scripture quotations marked NKJV are taken from the New King James Version®. © 1982 by Thomas Nelson. Used by permission. All rights reserved. Scripture quotations marked NLT are taken from the Holy Bible, New Living Translation. © 1996, 2004, 2015 by Tyndale House Foundation. Used by permission of Tyndale House Ministries, Carol Stream, Illinois 60188. All rights reserved. Scripture quotations marked THE VOICE are taken from The Voice™. © 2012 by Ecclesia Bible Society. Used by permission. All rights reserved. Scripture quotations marked TPT are taken from The Passion Translation®. © 2017, 2018 by Passion & Fire Ministries, Inc. Used by permission. All rights reserved. ThePassionTranslation.com.

Any internet addresses, phone numbers, or company or product information printed in this book are offered as a resource and are not intended in any way to be or to imply an endorsement by Thomas Nelson, nor does Thomas Nelson vouch for the existence, content, or services of these sites, phone numbers, companies, or products beyond the life of this book.

Library of Congress Cataloging-in-Publication Data

Names: McNeilly, Trina, 1977- author.
Title: Unclutter your soul : overcome what overwhelms you / Trina McNeilly.
Description: Nashville, Tennessee : W Publishing Group, an imprint of Thomas Nelson, [2022] | Includes bibliographical references.
Identifiers: LCCN 2021050484 (print) | LCCN 2021050485 (ebook) | ISBN 9780785250005 (paperback) | ISBN 9780785250593 (ebook)
Subjects: LCSH: Simplicity—Religious aspects—Christianity. | Thought and thinking—Religious aspects—Christianity. | Christianity—Psychology. | Spiritual life—Christianity.
Classification: LCC BV4647.S48 M39 2022 (print) | LCC BV4647.S48 (ebook) | DDC 248.4—dc23/eng/20211130
LC record available at https://lccn.loc.gov/2021050484
LC ebook record available at https://lccn.loc.gov/2021050485

Printed in the United States of America

24 25 26 27 28 LBC 7 6 5 4 3

For Stephen, who sees the way before
I write the story. I love you.

*I can't tell you how much I long for you
to enter this wide-open, spacious life.*
—2 Corinthians 6:11

CONTENTS

The Interior Design of Our Lives.. xi

PART 1: OBSERVE

1. Listen to the Soundtrack of Your Soul............................... 3
2. Accept a Custom Plan...13
3. Inventory Your Clutter...... 21
4. Pay Attention to Your Body 38
5. Know Your (Emotional) Age.................................47
6. Say Goodbye to Comfy Clutter.................................55
7. Don't Forget the Boxes in the Basement.........................63
8. Go Through to Get Out.................................72
9. Participate in Your Life.................................81
10. Imagine Space.................................88

PART 2: OWN

11. Tell Yourself the Truth.................................101
12. Embrace Mystery 111
13. Be a Thought Leader.................................119
14. Declare Your Decisions 126
15. Design New Patterns 133

Contents

16. Confess Your Expectations 141
17. Talk About the Things You Can't Talk About 148
18. Be at Home with Yourself.................................156

PART 3: OVERCOME

19. Tell Yourself a New Story................................163
20. Take Your Power Back 171
21. Trust God with Your Time 177
22. Pursue Peace...189
23. Engage to Find a Better Way 197
24. Nurture and Nourish....................................206
25. Ask for Help 218
26. See Everything As a Choice.............................226
27. Grow in Peace and Joy.................................236

A Bloom Is First a Bud 246

Acknowledgments 251

Notes...255

About the Author..263

THE INTERIOR DESIGN

OF OUR LIVES

The real voyage of discovery consists not in seeing new sights but in looking with new eyes.
—Marcel Proust[1]

Ten years ago my life seemed pretty put together. It wasn't perfect, by any means. I struggled with depression, which, at the time, I didn't fully understand. My husband was building a business, which led to stress in both our finances and marriage. I was newly pregnant with our fourth child and physically exhausted. There was also tension and dysfunction in my family of origin (isn't that normal?). Yet, amid the low hum of sadness and everyday stress, I felt secure. I could cope. There appeared to be order.

Then, on a day like any other, out of nowhere (so it seemed at the time), the smooth-enough seas turned turbulent and life as I knew it capsized.

My parents separated, which began an exhausting, stressful, lengthy divorce process. With the change of dynamics, I discovered almost immediately that my identity and security had not been rooted in Christ, as I had always assumed; rather it had been wrapped up in my family of origin.

It was as if the lid of Pandora's box had been lifted.

Dear grandparents began dying. We faced family addictions. I experienced a physical health scare and endured two events that I now understand to be traumas. And as if to sanction my unmooring, I left my beloved home (which also happened to be my childhood home).

There was disorder, and not just in my physical world. My inner home was also copiously cluttered.

There is a *living home* within you. Whether stately and beautiful, expansive and serene, or dilapidated and in disrepair, cluttered and chaotic—it's often hard to detect your own setting for lack of visibility. Especially today with all the external noise and distractions.

It's actually quite rare that someone doesn't have what I call *soul clutter*—the white noise of others' opinions, stories we tell ourselves to cope, lies we've believed or agreed with, unregulated emotions, or pain that has become paralyzing. It's also quite difficult to deal with the resulting chaos because either we cannot map a way beyond the clutter, or we are too afraid to journey into the thick of it.

This internal clutter takes its toll on a soul created for wide-open spaces. Soul clutter, if not addressed, can take on the forms of fear, depression, anxiety, addiction, chronic stress, and even physical ailments.

The low hum of disorder in my life had become a cacophony of stress and anxiety so that I was cluttered with

- loss,
- emotional pain,
- unhealthy coping mechanisms and behavioral patterns,
- chronic stress,
- crippling depression and anxiety,
- fear, and
- aversion to change.

I didn't understand it then, but this was the beginning of the journey of uncluttering my soul.

I don't blame my parents' divorce. It could have been another crisis. Eventually something else would have broken me. But this deconstructing became my catalyst to change. The origin. The genesis of my journey.

I didn't recognize it because of all the clutter. I was too close to it all, too closed in. No one recognizes the precipice of a soul pilgrimage. It feels nothing like movement, which is nothing short of a gift if you are paralyzed with heartbreak, change, anxiety, depression, and the like. But, Dear Reader, all journeys begin still.

I imagine you are a lot like me. You want your life to change for the better. You desire to grow and become the healthiest version of yourself—spirit, soul, and body. You are doing your best to discover and walk in your calling and purposes. Me too.

Yet no matter how much we want our lives to change, no matter how many steps we take in the right direction, we often find ourselves stuck or walking in circles continually facing the same obstacles. We have big feelings, and if we are intellectually honest with ourselves, then we are (or are becoming) aware that we also have behavioral patterns, coping mechanisms, perhaps even addictions that are cluttering our lives, confounding us, and keeping us from the change we so desire.

If we are alike, as I believe, then you, too, are willing to do the hard work (or you wouldn't be reading this!). We don't shy from starts and have learned to be steadfast in purpose. We won't capitulate without resistance. We are committed to "just keep moving," even if it feels like we are trudging through sludge or we have yet to take that first step in the direction of the life we long for. If we are not so different, I can be quite certain that you are tired and fatigued.

For more than a decade I've written extensively online sharing ideas and inspiration for creating beauty in our homes and our hearts. I've loved offering practical advice to create a beloved home as well as encouraging women to attend to the home that matters most—their hearts.

In my first book, *La La Lovely*, I helped readers find the beauty in their everyday lives, no matter what they were going through. I found beauty to be an answer to my ache (my brokenness and pain). But the answer didn't stop with beauty. As I was putting the finishing touches on my first book, I found myself living out the book you are holding. I had become an expert at adding all things lovely to life (and advising others to do so), but now I was having to sort through and let go of the unlovely things.

I've spent years quietly learning (through personal experience, process, and research) how to unclutter my own soul. I'm ready to share my story and guide you through this space-making process. My journey is not complete. I share my experiences with you as a fellow traveler. As someone who is putting one foot in front of the other, unpacking one box at a time, owning and overcoming— doing the hard work alongside you. And by the way, please note that while I make a great traveling companion and guide, I am not a licensed therapist, and this book in no way is a substitute for, or should be treated as, professional help. I advocate and personally practice seeking professional help when needed.

Picture me as the big sister or friend who you call up when you are utterly overwhelmed (on the verge of a meltdown). The one you call when you don't know what to do or where to begin. The one you call when you don't want to go it alone. With grace, hope, and humor, together we will get into the mess of life to get out of it. We'll sort through and get rid of the things holding you down and holding you back. We'll work together to clean up and clear out—to create the space that your soul craves.

Now, tell me.

> *Do you ever feel as if your inner life is tight, busy, or chaotic?*
> *Are your emotions calling all the shots?*
> *Do you find yourself the owner of an overactive mind, often leaving*
>   *you paralyzed from moving forward and living life to the fullest?*
> *Perhaps you are doing "all the things" yet feeling as if it's never*
>   *enough, and that you're not making progress?*
> *Are you unaware of how or where to begin?*

If so, then I invite you to take this journey with me. With the torchlight of God's love leading, we will navigate through the highs and lows of your internal abode—your very own unique design—and into the home of your heart and soul (your mind, will, and emotions) where the clutter resides.

Together, with the Holy Spirit as our guide, we will start on a journey of three stages. First, in part one we'll acknowledge the clutter (Observe). To see the mess before us, we have to open our eyes, even though it can be overwhelming. Then we'll make space for a healthy internal environment (Own). We'll own all our junk and feel the freedom that comes with taking action. Finally, in part three we'll uncover tools for living clutter-free from the inside out (Overcome), with a plan forward and the goal of peaceful, spacious, open living in your soul.

Your soul was created for wide-open spaces (for a kingdom within!). Emotional pain, stress, anxiety, and depression no longer need to crowd or control your life. Transformation is possible.

Through sharing my personal journey along with truths in Scripture, practical advice, daily practices, and Create Space activities at the end of each chapter, you'll learn to identify clutter, release mindsets, redirect thoughts, regulate emotions, and begin creating space and new inward paths that will lead you to peace and joy in *your* everyday life.

Open the windows, turn on the hall lights. We're going to get into every closet and cabinet, nook and cranny. We'll enter crawl spaces and basements with care. With intention and purpose we will clear out and let go of what no longer serves us, creating a beautiful and spacious place within.

This is the genesis of your journey.

Part one
Observe

When we devote no time to the inner life, we lose the habit of soul. If we fail to acquaint ourselves with soul, we will remain strangers in our own lives.
—John O'Donohue[1]

1

LISTEN TO THE SOUNDTRACK

OF YOUR SOUL

Until you make the unconscious conscious, it will
direct your life and you will call it fate.
—Carl Jung[1]

I love a good soundtrack.

On any given day, to the sound of movie music, I'm Elizabeth Bennett, heady and floating through the fields just beyond Netherfield. I'm Kathleen Kelly walking to the Shop Around the Corner on a crisp autumn day in New York City. I'm fifteen again, angsty and curled up in my waterbed, emoting to the *Edward Scissorhands* soundtrack booming on my double cassette stereo. Or I'm me, now—fortysomething, dancing in the kitchen with my family to *Mamma Mia!* and, admittedly, envisioning myself as Donna (cool '70s vibe included) on a Greek island (*sigh*) as I belt out "Super Trouper" (a family theme song of sorts) in my best Cher vibrato.

With songs and soundtracks, I feel it all. I feel melancholy and pain. I feel hope and joy. I feel other-ly and myself all the same. I feel possibility, inspiration, and imagination at work.

You may have guessed by now that a few of my all-time favorite soundtracks include *You've Got Mail, Pride and Prejudice, Mamma Mia!,* and *Edward Scissorhands.* They are my favorites because they make me feel *something*!

I also tend to create a soundtrack for my life. You know how this works. You hear a song on the radio or playlist and instantly you are struck with emotion. A time. A place. A person. You feel what you felt *then* ("Ice Ice Baby" = eighth grade! *Anyone?*).

Well, Dear Reader, your soul has a soundtrack, even if you've never recognized it as such. It could be a playlist of pain. Perhaps chronic stress, like static you can't tune out. The low hum of white noise akin to anxiety. Maybe there is silence where you are aching to hear something, anything. Possibly your soundtrack is an ever-shifting eclectic mix of happy and sad tunes.

Your soul is speaking.

The World Health Organization reports that globally more than 264 million people suffer from depression[2] and one in thirteen suffers from anxiety—the most common of mental disorders worldwide.[3] The National Survey on Drug Use and Health stated in their 2018 report that in America alone 20.3 million people (twelve years and older) battled a substance disorder.[4] With these statistics it is evident that we have an epidemic of souls overwhelmed with damaged emotions and pain. Millions are suffering, unaware of how to heal, and finding themselves in a spectrum of behaviors to cope. The spectrum can range from numbing out by mindless scrolling on Instagram to anesthetizing with substances.

No matter how loud or languid, *your* soul is playing a tune.

Whether joyful or despondent, it's telling a tale and offering precious information that is elemental for change. It's time we stopped turning down the volume, skipping to the next song, or completely zoning out while a pain playlist is set to repeat. Now is the time to begin listening. Today is the day to start truly paying attention to the soundtrack of your soul.

I wasn't listening to my soul. It was Christmas 2013, and I was completely resisting the fact that my parents were newly separated after nearly forty years of marriage. Relationships in my family of origin were swiftly shifting, and I was left confounded and wounded. Then, unexpectedly, days before Christmas, my thirty-one-year-old cousin passed away. Everything felt dark and irreparable during a season in which we had always celebrated and experienced peace and joy. I was overwhelmed with emotional pain, but I couldn't name it as such. I would have told you I was sad, maybe depressed, depending on the day. Looking back, I knew I was confused, scared, uncertain, exhausted, and facing chronic stress, but I couldn't see beyond the burning emotion in the moment.

On one of those cold, dark December nights I was forced to begin paying attention to my soul. Having just left the hotel where my grandma and aunt were staying for the funeral, I was driving myself home. It was a quiet moment, at first (the empty car being a sanctuary for moms with young children, *right?!*). Knowing the roads like the back of my hand, I was driving on autopilot and turned up the music in an attempt to drown out my weighty thoughts. Thoughts that morphed into something of a singular conversation— okay, argument—with myself. I debated why I should or should not drive straight to O'Hare, hop on a plane, and take off to anywhere. As I argued out loud with myself, I began to ugly cry.

The next thing I knew, I was pounding on the steering wheel and screaming at the top of my lungs—guttural screaming (revisiting this moment now still evokes emotion). After my private tirade concluded, I sat still in shock. I make no promise of not being an emotional and sometimes dramatic person (Enneagram Four here); however, I had no idea where that heated outburst had come from.

In hindsight I understand that there was a lot going on in my soul—a major storm was brewing. Yet in the moment I was shocked that I had had such a primal physical reaction. I was taken aback because I detected anger. By nature, I'm not an angry person. It has never been a typical response of mine. But there I was, seething with anger, in my SUV: my throat scratchy from screaming, my entire body hot with indignation. I'd be remiss if I didn't tell you that I've had more of those heated moments since.

My pain—my anger—was trying to tell me something. The soundtrack of my soul was overriding the surface data.

One way or another, pain will get you to pay attention. Paying attention to what your pain is telling you, however, is an entirely different thing.

What Exactly Is Your Soul?

What do you imagine your soul looks like? For better or worse my mind is imaginative. I see in stories, colors, layers, characters, and spaces. In fact much of my personal uncluttering work has been to reframe the "worse" part of my imagination—to get my mind to work *for* me rather than *against* me. Therefore, I can't help but see my inner life as a place. A home. After all, it is a dwelling place for our soul and spirit, as well as the Spirit of God (should we invite Him in). Throughout Scripture we see references to Christ abiding and dwelling within.[5] Jesus tells His followers, "Live in me. Make your home in me *just as I do in you*" (John 15:4, emphasis mine). In the New Testament believers are described as a sanctuary or temple; we are the place in which the Spirit of God makes His permanent home.[6] This means we hold an entire kingdom within.

For a moment, close your eyes and imagine with me.

A place.

A landscape.

A home.

A kingdom!

Can you see it?

We are not mere flesh and bones. We are living homes.

We are not mere matter. We are ever-broadening containers.

With this beautiful picture in mind, I now want to lay a foundation before we begin our journey. I want to be clear about defining what our soul is. The word *soul* is often used to describe who a person really is—the nonphysical part, their spiritual nature. Often "soul" is used in the same manner as "heart" or "spirit," but let's take a closer look.

When I was growing up, my dad taught me that "I am a spirit, I have a soul, and I live in a body."[7] This gave me a wonderful framework, which I'm grateful for; yet it's only now that I'm beginning to understand the differentiation of the spirit, soul, and body. Differentiation and connectedness, that is. All components work together, and each affects the others.

Your body is your physical nature, the exterior. It is the structure of the home in which your spirit and your soul reside. Your spirit is the eternal you—the true you. It is your God-breathed life according to Genesis 2:7. Our soul, often confused or sometimes used interchangeably with *spirit*, is composed of our mind, will, and emotions (which is what I'll be referring to as I use the word *soul* throughout this book).

Scripture says that in Christ we become new creatures, meaning our spirit is instantaneously made new (2 Corinthians 5:17). Yet it is our soul (our mind, will, and emotions) that needs constant renewing (Ephesians 4:23–24 AMP). The renewing is what transforms our lives (Romans 12:2).

Renewing requires our participation.

Won't you join me in participating in your own renewal?

Observing Is Participation

Let's begin our participation by *observing*.

One of the first steps to clearing out clutter is to become a student of yourself: the moments that force your attention but also, and most importantly, your everyday life. Our lives have patterns, and so do our thoughts. Like the weather. Like terrain. Like how we pile clutter. We must begin to pay attention not only to our pain but also to our beliefs, habits, choices, behaviors, responses, patterns, and outcomes. It goes beyond making a list of our strengths and weaknesses and takes us into the territory of *why* we react, respond, and behave as we do. When we know the why, we can accept grace from God as well as ourselves.

Your soul is speaking.

Your emotions are trying to tell you something.

Your anger.

Your sadness.

Your fear.

Your surprise.

Your joy.

Your grief.

Your clutter.

They are not to be ignored, quickly dismissed, or even judged at this time. Simply observe. Try as you may to silence unwelcome or unruly emotions, they will only get louder. You can attempt to ignore the clutter, but it will continue to multiply, take up space, and close in on you.

Perhaps you are already in the process of paying attention and you have an idea of what your soul is trying to tell you. Or maybe you can't yet see what is inside of you or right in front of you. Don't be discouraged by what you find or cannot find. Paying attention is a process. Observing takes time.

And it starts with simply being still. It begins with looking around and taking in all your surroundings. Noticing what's been neglected, what hasn't been working, what you've been avoiding.

As I mentioned, all journeys begin still. And to be fair, I should warn you that this is not a smooth sailing, linear journey. There are many starts and stops. We aren't just hiring a dumpster to clean out the neglected basement, storage unit, or crawl space in a day. There is much assessing and sorting to be done in this space-making process. And, contrary as it sounds, stillness is an indispensable component of movement. So as we progress, if we pause, I want you to see stops and stillness as super boosts, although they may feel or appear to be anything but.

Sitting in this kind of stillness is anything but inactivity because *paying attention precedes change.* When we become aware of *why* we want to change and *what* needs to change, the natural progression then is to change. And with the help of the Holy Spirit, we can make lasting change, one step at a time.

Let's take a moment to breathe deeply and be still. In this pause, hope is available if we will ask the Spirit to flood our hearts, the center of our beings, with light. This is not elusive, wishful hope. This is a hope that we can know and understand, a hope we are called to (Ephesians 1:18).

For the moment tune out all other voices. There are so many well-meaning voices in our lives and in our minds. The ones we've

> *Paying attention precedes change. When we become aware of why we want to change and what needs to change, the natural progression then is to change.*

sought out for wisdom and advice. The ones that have given an opinion or assessment of your situation (whether warranted or not). The voice in your mind that is judgmental, bossy, or opinionated about your life. (I wonder, does this voice have a tone? Does the inflection or verbiage sound familiar? Like a parent? Grandparent? A former leader, boss, or person of authority? Maybe it's the sound of your own voice—a perfectionistic pitch—ever critical of your efforts or lack thereof.) Quiet them all.

Now, what do you hear?

If you can't hear, what do you feel?

If there are no words, are there tears? Are there physical reactions?

If you can't articulate, do you scream or shut down? Do you run to an activity?

If you can't feel, have you made yourself numb? Do you distract yourself?

That anger outburst in my car, many Christmases ago, was my soul howling: *Pay attention!* Since then, my soul has sent out a number of SOS signals—some extravagant, others ever so subtle—all inviting me to pay attention to the state of my inner life and participate in the renewing of my soul.

I imagine your soul is extending an invitation to you: *Come along, I've got a plan.*

To help you through this uncluttering journey, I encourage you to sit and take time with the Create Space section at the end of each chapter. I've written this as a guide, giving you space to pause and reflect, as well as providing practical action steps you can take to ignite growth and change. Wherever you are in the process, experiencing more room or buried in clutter, this section will encourage you, keep you on course, and help you make the space-making progress you desire.

CREATE SPACE

Meditate

I encourage you not only to read these scriptures but to engage with them, meditate on them:

1. Read the text slowly (Is there a word you want to research?)
2. Imagine it (I envision what I'm reading. I picture myself doing what the Word says.)
3. Read it aloud (Hearing God's Word builds our faith, according to Romans 10.17.)
4. Reflect and listen (What is God revealing, speaking to me?)

Do not conform to the pattern of this world, but be transformed by the renewing of your mind. Then you will be able to test and approve what God's will is—his good, pleasing and perfect will.
—ROMANS 12:2 NIV

For a more extensive list of promises to meditate on, visit
trinamcneilly.com/unclutterpromises

Reflect

These reflection questions will help you get the most out of *Uncluttering Your Soul*. Consider keeping a companion journal or notebook nearby to chronicle your process and progress. You'll be amazed at the insight you uncover if you'll take time to reflect and respond.

1. What emotions keep surfacing in your life?
2. Do you have a propensity to ignore or numb your pain?
3. What is your soul trying to tell you?

Act

Let's put what we are learning into practice. As I've mentioned, paying attention (observing) precedes change. Yet even when we are ready and willing, sometimes we just don't know where or how to begin. That's why I've created small actionable steps to help you activate change. Sometimes you'll see a prayer and other times a practical exercise. Don't worry, I'm not going to add more overwhelm—I'm here to help you overcome it!

Pray this prayer:

Lord, You know me better than I know myself. I ask that You illuminate the eyes of my imagination and show me what I've been avoiding and what I cannot yet see. Help me not to fear the journey, but rather to take courage as we forge ahead and sort through the clutter together. Thank You for healing my pain and for peace and joy that are available to me every step of the way. Amen.

2

ACCEPT A CUSTOM PLAN

*Sometimes the process of growth looks a lot like
destruction and pain. But you'll realize with time
that you're not breaking, you're healing.*
—Brittany Burgunder[1]

Have you seen the popular show *Tidying Up with Marie Kondo* on Netflix? Marie Kondo is the darling Japanese decluttering guru who comes into people's homes and helps them rid their homes of clutter—sorting through and organizing everything *all at once*. Ruthlessly and joyfully (what a combination) they eliminate anything that is not useful or does not spark joy.

The show is a brilliant visual to the strategies and stories she outlined in her book; it gives us a front-row seat to just how this wild concept of taking everything out of its space—all at once—to assess each and every piece really works. "Does this serve a purpose?" "Does this spark joy?" If the answer is no, then Marie says thank the clothing, the object, the utensil, and then let it go. Only the necessary items and the ones that spark joy return to their respective homes—the closet, the drawer, the basement.

I confess, I like to watch this process. I'm up for the task in my mind's eye, but I haven't yet tried it. While intriguing, it's always felt extreme. Maybe if Marie were there to hold my hand, I could take the plunge. People everywhere are trying, however, because her method has become so popular it's been given a name and trade-marked: the KonMari Method.

At the onset of the Marie Kondo craze, I was working on my own method of ridding my life of clutter—uncluttering my soul. I, too, was doing the messy work of eliminating my own objects of familiarity that were taking up space, serving no purpose, and weighing me down. I, too, wanted to rid my life of anything that did not spark joy.

Here's the part I imagine that you're waiting for. My formula. The exact step-by-step method. Before-and-after photos, the kind we are accustomed to seeing on our screens as we swipe every single day. The "Ten Ways to Change Your Life" PDF download that costs you only your email address. The cheat sheet. The bonus to boost your results.

The promise of magic.

Are you ready? You might need to sit down.

Here it is.

My method is this: There is no method. There is no fail-proof formula.

There is, however, a custom plan. And there are promises. They are not my promises, thankfully. They are promises of freedom, space for your soul to breathe, peace, and joy—sealed by the Holy Spirit—outlined in God's unfailing Word.

I want to offer you magic—in this book's title, in the method. I want to offer you the fast track. I'd love the ten fail-proof steps too. But, Dear Reader, I cannot promise you magic. There are far more than ten steps; there is a beautiful winding path. I want to point you in that direction.

The chapter titles of this book are action oriented because, through years and years of overthinking, I'm learning that action activates change (faith without works is dead[2]). Over and over I'm brought back to the verse in Psalm 37:23 (AMP) that says, "The *steps* of a [good and righteous] man are directed and established by the LORD, and He delights in his way [and blesses his path]" (emphasis mine). If we aren't taking steps, how can we be directed? In this book I'm sharing my stories, my process, the steps I've taken. Count me as a traveling companion, a big sister, a guide pointing you to the way.

This is not magic; it is holy work.

It would be great if you could KonMari your mind and emotions—to sort through everything *all at once*—but soul clutter can't be cleared that way. While there are biblical truths, principles, and directions that are universal to us all, the Father asks us each to keep in step with the Spirit.

The process is personal; the plan is custom.

I can't help but think of custom-made closets. You know the kind: gorgeous with beautiful built-in shelving, velvet-covered hangers, a full-length, gilded mirror propped unpretentiously against the wall, a sofa or seat in the center. God, the great organizer of our life, is not asking us to make a Target run and schlep random organizing shelves and bins into an overflowing cart. No, He is Creator and Carpenter, and He

Action activates change.

15

is creating and building a custom plan for *your* needs. I may need more space for sweaters, you for sundresses. I may need drawers and you need baskets. God knows our needs; He has the design.

A few summers ago I tried a twenty-one-day vegan program. This choice wasn't based on a desire to become vegan. I mean, I love vegetables, and I'm always working to eat my thirty different plant-based foods per week (research shows this is optimal for gut health[3]), but I also love me some meat. Red meat. All my friends know that I love a good cheeseburger (and my besties know I even like a crappy one from McDonald's every now and again). I'm from the Midwest, after all.

For me, this was yet another program that might have the answers I sought. It seemed like it had worked magic for the people I read about in the reviews. The founder of the program, Kris Carr, has a remarkable story of healing from cancer. At the time I was regularly breaking out in hives. I'd scratch my legs all through the night, using all my willpower not to freak out when I looked in the mirror because it reminded me of a time that I became extremely ill from an antibiotic reaction. I thought that if I eliminated certain foods from my diet and ate really clean, something would happen, something would change. I was looking for answers by way of elimination. And I was hoping for results. Per usual, I was looking for a magic bullet.

The program took a lot of work and discipline. You cannot even imagine the shopping and prep required. On top of that I continued regular meals for the boys, who only participated by saying "Eww, gross" at every meal—the encouragement was so helpful. Ella, my oldest, joined me in this endeavor, which was fun except that she, too, joined in on the "Eww, gross" chorus for most meals. But she stuck to it. She did it. We did it.

Smack in the middle of the program we were invited by a friend to attend the local country club's Fourth of July celebration. The kids could swim, and there were rides, a lovely meal, and fireworks. As we were waiting in line to get tickets for the rides, I noticed a few familiar faces that I was not expecting to see. People I preferred to be prepared to see. There was no avoiding one another, only time for a quick prayer for grace and a deep breath before "Oh, hi!" Okay, there was no deep breathing. There was heart pounding and shortness of breath.

Before I knew it, "Hello, how are you?" turned into lunching together. In the dining room, under the round table cloaked in a crisp country-club tablecloth, I began itching like a shaggy dog. As we all emerged into the sunlight, there was no hiding my red, blotchy, scratched-up legs that gave the appearance I had been attacked by a rabid animal.

It turns out, hives weren't necessarily about the food I was eating; they were about the stress I was encountering.

The process of following that program gave me insight about myself as well as the path that I'm on—even as it pertains to how I eat. The two greatest findings I took away had nothing to do with food. They had to do with stress and perfectionism: I gained a clearer understanding that stress seems to be the major culprit of my physical issue and that I need to focus on progress, not perfection. I began to live by the words repeated over and over again in the program: "progress over perfection." I found great relief in discovering that there was grace and space for imperfection.

Just as one type of diet or food protocol doesn't work for every body because everybody is unique, so it is with our souls. That is not to say that there are not truths and principles that are good for everybody, because there are. The more I talk with people who are overcoming and finding freedom, the more I notice patterns and similarities. Light that lets us know we are not traveling alone. Light that shows us we are headed in the right direction or, perhaps, the wrong direction. Light that we are then able to shine in the direction of others' darkness. Our stories and journeys are different, yet strangely there is sameness. I believe as you continue reading these pages, you will have this experience. A trace at the turn of the pages. A place in the plot of my stories. For while we are intricately unique and our details differ, the pain, the progress, the purpose share both a human and divine thread.

Death. Addiction. Loss. Abandonment. Illness. Financial loss. Failure. Depression. Divorce. Anxiety. Your version may materialize differently, but this we share.

Hope. Light. Salvation. Healing. Freedom. Your path may differ, but this we share.

Somewhere along the way, in all my effort to be proactive in uncluttering by observing, and with my propensity to look for a magic bullet, the Lord reminded me of His custom plan for my life with these words:

> *You are paying too much attention to what other people are doing. Paying attention to how they are doing it may be one thing, but I want you to be aware of overly observing to compare what you are not doing. I don't want you to pay attention to their pace. I want you to pay attention to our pace—to Me. Follow Me. Two words that weren't just said for salvation—but for your life, your everyday life. In your every movement, action, thought, decision, reaction, response, motivation, and creation, follow Me.*
>
> *Not parents. Not culture. Not successful people with their three-step plans. Not well-intentioned friends. Not ideals. Not expectations. Not "supposed-to-be's." Follow Me. If there is someone I want you to learn from, I will lead you to them or them to you. There will be people I place in your path (for your benefit*

or theirs). People who are further along to light the way and also people for you to walk alongside or lead. I will spur the connection on or direct you on how to do this. Follow Me. This is not about being a go-getter or lack of hustling. This is about kingdom living and you, dear daughter, are learning the Way. I'm not unclear nor withholding. Follow Me. Most believe this to be too simple; therefore, they create their own way. I've got your five-year plan. Follow Me. I am the Way.

My method is this: it's your method—custom built by the Great Designer of your life.

I will leave you with a process found in Psalm 55:16–17 that is for each and every one of us:

1. Call upon the Lord to save you and know that He will.
2. Every morning move your soul toward Him.
3. Every evening explain your need to Him.
4. Every evening explain your need to Him.

There is a promise attached to this process: He will hear and respond to your cry.

I wrote these words on a fluorescent sticky note and stuck it on the side of my nightstand so that I would see (observe) them before I drifted off to sleep and first thing upon the dawn of a new day.

To continue with a custom plan, you'll need to take an inventory of your clutter. In this next chapter we'll delve into various types of soul clutter. As you observe, you'll begin to discover what particular clutter is overwhelming *your* life. Although it may look like we've just emptied out your entire closet only to clutter up your bedroom, be encouraged these observations will provide the clarity you need to begin to own and overcome.

CREATE SPACE

Meditate

Now since we have chosen to walk with the Spirit, let's keep each step in perfect sync with God's Spirit.

—GALATIANS 5:25 THE VOICE

Reflect

1. Do you find yourself eager to fix everything all at once? Could you give yourself permission to celebrate progress?
2. Are you more prone to figuring out and forging your own way or following others?
3. Are you willing to take a step, and let the Lord lead?

Act

Pray this prayer:

Father, I want Your custom plan and path for my life. You know my deepest desires and my needs. You know what needs reorganizing and what needs to go, entirely. Continue to shine Your love into the unlit corners of my heart and soul. Lead me to the right programs, people, professionals, books, messages, music, art, and movement that will help me to make progress. Help me not to put my hope in these things or in the promise of people but to continually remember that my hope is anchored in You. May I always keep in step with the Spirit. Help me to step away from the illusion of perfection and embrace the process. Open my eyes to progress and teach me to celebrate the newly created space in my soul. Amen.

3

INVENTORY YOUR CLUTTER

—⁓—

When we are no longer able to change a situation,
we are challenged to change ourselves.
—Viktor Frankl[1]

Take a look at your surroundings. Literally. Cars bustling by. People rushing about, heads down and eyes glued to their glowing screens. Earphones always in—a podcast or pundit chattering. Blinking billboards with deals. Twenty-four-hour news and talking heads. Texting, email, social media, and a phone that FaceTimes. Amazon and Google. Advertisements for pharmaceuticals besieging your screens—making you leery of your own body. And this is but a glimpse at the exterior noise.

Inside, we might not be able to name or identify the noise and clutter quite as clearly. It's a low hum. A curmudgeon of a companion. An ache. A pattern. An unaddressed symptom or pain. Unnamed. Repetitive and yet repeatedly ignored.

The first step in any recovery is acknowledging that there is a problem. How can we clean or make space if we can't first acknowledge that there is clutter?

Identifying our soul clutter is not anything to be ashamed of. I hope to help demystify the shame of an overactive mind and validate its brilliance and great purpose.

Before we can progress in uncluttering, we first must pay attention to the pain and identify the problem. Paying attention can be a slow process easily discounted by impatience. I have found it's worth taking the time because paying attention is a great teacher if we will submit ourselves as students; it often yields both the equation and the answer.

Let's take inventory. Here's how I did it.

It's fall, nearly a year after my acquaintance with anger, and I'm walking through my wooded neighborhood admiring the leaves: marigold, scarlet, and bronze. Their sound, crunchy and crackling, always gets my attention. In my ears "The Secret Life of Daydreams" (isn't that the best title ever?) is competing with the crunch. It's an instrumental piece, which gives my mind room to think and my soul space to speak. When I listen between the crunch and the crackle, I hear the whimpers of pain; my daydream is always to escape.

I returned to my house, nestled in the trees, to find a package from my grandma—one of her soul-care packages, as I'd later learn to call them. Each box, posted from Colorado, contained books, notes, and trinkets that made her think of me—her granddaughter, now dubbed her student.

This particular package included a book titled *Healing for Damaged Emotions*.[2] My custom was to always do a quick flip through, scanning for her red-pen underlines and handwritten notes, which, if I was lucky enough to find, brought instant comfort like a warm cup of tea on a bone-cold winter's day. I remember thinking, *Well, this one isn't for me; I don't have damaged emotions.* I closed the book and gingerly tucked it on my shelf. I'd still want to keep it close, in sight, as I would a newborn in a bassinet.

The pain was loud—I could hear it, like the leaves, like the song. And although I was beginning to be able to put a name to it, I was still too close to understand what it was doing in my body and soul—how it was the source of many issues I was facing.

These days as I attend to my clutter, I'm having to sort through layers. Within each box and bin are layers of items, rolled in tissue paper, bundled in bubble wrap. For instance, when I began to unpack stress, within that box I also dug out overwhelm, everyday stress, and chronic stress—all remnants that had to be dealt with.

To help you inventory your clutter, I'm sharing some of my major culprits, many of which I'm sorting through right alongside you. An entire book could be written on each type of clutter, so it's important to understand that this next section is an overview for the purpose of observing. In subsequent chapters I give you practical resources, along with my stories of observing, owning, and overcoming these types of clutter, to keep you company and shine a light as we journey on.

Perhaps you will identify a type of soul clutter that I have not listed—this is not an exhaustive list. I trust that the Holy Spirit will reveal what needs revealing today and also that He will bring you back to this section for continued reviewing and revealing (spoiler alert: that is how clearing out the clutter and creating space works; it's a continued process).

When you're decluttering your house, you might take advice

from organization gurus and make a list of rooms—bedroom, bathroom, living room. Then you might identify the boxes of clutter within each room and reflect on how those function (or don't function, as the case may be). You may identify how you *wish* they would function. But first you must open the door to the room and take a long, hard look at what's inside. The illustrated boxes on the next page may look scary or overwhelming, but they have something to tell you if you look inside. We have to see something before we can clear it out; we have to name it to find freedom from it. As we go through each of these subcategories together, we'll explore them in the bright light of day. Then you'll know what you're dealing with. Remember, nothing about this uncluttering process requires perfection or speed. The pace is yours. It's your custom plan; it's a process you can return to.

And now let's look at each category and see what there is to see, eyes and heart wide open.

Types of Clutter

Fear: Worry and Anxiety

What makes you afraid? As far back as I can remember, I've always been prone to being afraid. I really hate admitting this because as a believer I don't want to be in fear; after all, "fear not" is a command. But if we look at the definition of *fear*, "an unpleasant often strong emotion caused by anticipation or awareness of danger,"[3] we can see that fear is also an emotion. Like anger, like happiness, like sadness. When I view fear in that paradigm, I'm not bordered within the confines of condemnation. It reminds me of when the apostle Paul said, "Be angry, and do not sin" (Ephesians 4:26 NKJV). I always try to remember, too, that fear can serve as a warning.

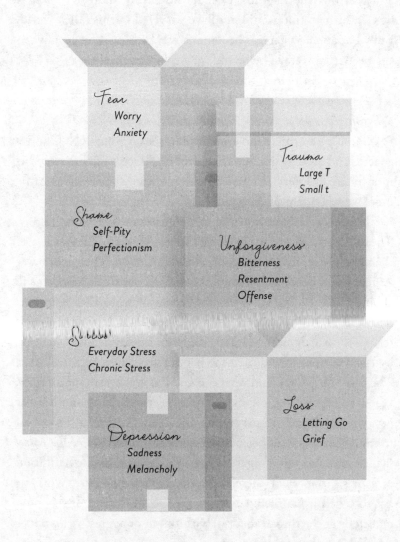

Fear
Worry
Anxiety

Trauma
Large T
Small t

Shame
Self-Pity
Perfectionism

Unforgiveness
Bitterness
Resentment
Offense

Stress
Everyday Stress
Chronic Stress

Loss
Letting Go
Grief

Depression
Sadness
Melancholy

Other types of clutter, some of which are mentioned later in the book, may include loneliness, discouragement, anger, powerlessness, hurt, rejection, and disappointment. As mentioned, this is not an exhaustive list of soul clutter.

Without the emotion of fear indicating danger ("*Run!* A lion!"), humankind would not have survived in this fallen world. But what about when fear becomes a way of life? When we live in the perpetual state of believing we are in danger?

Do you find yourself perpetually afraid?

Perhaps there is a valid, underlying reason why you are fearful. What might it be?

Some of us (my hand's up) worry like it's our job. Like it's genetic and entirely out of our control (we'll look further into this in a future chapter). Like it's a noble concern, believing that the more we worry, the more we care.

I observed a lot of worry from the maternal side of my family. These were the most caring people I've ever known. They were also the most tied-up-in-knots people I've ever known. There was never a time when there wasn't something or someone to be "concerned" about.

When I was growing up, my mom would watch Joyce Meyer on television (which meant I watched Joyce). I'll never forget walking by the television one day to see her teaching in a rocking chair. The topic was worry, and what she said has stuck with me all these years: "Worry is like a rocking chair: it keeps you busy, but it never gets you anywhere." In my teens I dug deeper into what Joyce had to say about worry in her bestselling book *Battlefield of the Mind* (which was a game changer for me). She notes that one definition of *worry* is to torment oneself with disturbing thoughts.[4] Worry as a verb is defined as such: "to harass by tearing, biting, or snapping especially at the throat; to assail with rough or aggressive attack or treatment: *torment*."[5]

It's hard to believe worry is care and concern when we can now observe it as harassment, aggression, and torment. And that's exactly what it feels like after I spend any good amount of time worrying. Worn out, sick stomach, utterly attacked. The Enemy of our souls uses worry to wear us down, harass us, and torment us. Worrying requires extensive energy and does not yield results.

Let's pay attention to the word *anticipate* (remember, fear can be an "emotion caused by anticipation or awareness of danger"), which can be defined as "expectation or hope."[6] Worrying, then, is the act of putting our expectation and hope into a distressing possibility rather than putting our faith in a good God.

Do you notice yourself mistaking worry for care or concern?

Anxiety is such a buzzword and can be defined a number of ways. In general, anxiety is the body's natural response to stress.[7] It's a feeling of fear or apprehension about what's to come. I once heard a doctor explain that anxiety comes from the thinking part of the brain (which surprised me). He explained further that our brain tries to predict what is going to happen in the future based on past experiences, and when it can't predict, that's when anxiety sets in.[8]

> Worrying, then, is the act of putting our expectation and hope into a distressing possibility rather than putting our faith in a good God.

In addition to the anxieties of everyday life, many of us suffer from more intense anxiety, whether it is general anxiety, anxiety disorder, or anxiety attacks.* In my own experience with anxiety, I've learned that it can manifest differently for different people though it may show common attributes. For me, anxiety has looked like shortness of breath, stomachaches, fatigue, and sweating (that's fun to talk about).

In chatting with friends about panic attacks, I've found our

---

* The Anxiety and Depression Association of America reports that anxiety disorders are the most common mental illness in the US, affecting 40 million adults in the United States ages eighteen and older, or 18.1 percent of the population every year. "Facts and Statistics," ADAA, last updated April 21, 2021, https://adaa.org/understanding-anxiety/facts-statistics.

experiences to vary. One friend described her experience as heart palpitations, shortness of breath, and chest pain. I experienced shortness of breath, chills, pins and needles in my extremities, and trembling. On one occasion my tremors were so intense I ended up in the ER, believing something was seriously wrong with me. After the doctors ran tests, they wrote it up as anxiety. I had a hard time taking their word for it because it didn't look like what I thought a panic attack looked like. Yet after further symptoms and experiencing the same symptoms again, I now know that this is how my body responds to extreme stress and anxiety.

Do you notice a pattern in how your body responds to anxiety? Does anxiety affect your daily life?

Stress: Everyday and Chronic

Anxiety and stress are closely related—like siblings almost always together. Stress is our body's reaction to pressure and demands; it causes tension mentally, emotionally, and physically. The Mayo Clinic describes stress as both "acute" (which I like to call everyday stress) and "chronic." Acute stress is defined as your body's immediate reaction to a perceived threat, challenge, or scare. Chronic stress, however, is persistent. It is described as more subtle, and it can be more problematic as the effect may be long term.[9] According to the World Health Organization, stress has been classified as the health epidemic of the twenty-first century.[10]

Everyday stress looks like taking a test, juggling a busy workload, getting stuck in a traffic jam, giving a presentation, or meeting a deadline. I found it really helpful to understand that stress is a part of our lives and that not all stress is negative. When we have a stress response, our bodies release the stress hormone cortisol, which is designed to give us a spurt of energy. (A lion! Run!) Cortisol spikes, and then it should drop. However, when we are in a state of constant stress, our cortisol levels don't regulate—this is when stress becomes dangerous.

One way to tell if you might be experiencing chronic stress is to pay attention to when you experience a natural stressor, like having to brake quickly for a red light or hearing a noise in the middle of the night. Are you able to regulate back to a normal state? How long does it take you to calm down? When we have chronic stress, we become unable to deal with everyday stress. The lines become blurred. The dog pees on the carpet, and it's as if the world is coming to an end. If you stay in a state of high alert and find yourself transferring that stress onto other situations, you may be dealing with chronic stress. If you have a long-term stressor, such as chronic illness, financial issues, or divorce, you may be dealing with chronic stress. It's important to identify as it can progressively weaken the prefrontal cortex and affect our recovery from everyday episodes of stress.[11]

Are you on edge all the time? Do you jump or startle at loud noises that don't seem to bother others?

Are situations and stressors in your life running you?

Loss: Grief and Letting Go

Loss, letting go, and grief are inescapable. When we think of grief, we naturally think of physical death. However, grief can also be ambiguous. Consider when there is loss of something other-ly (a relationship, a home, a season, a way of life). In these cases you might not even recognize that you are experiencing grief.

Several years ago Stephen and I traveled to Colorado for a marriage intensive. I was personally in the throes of sadness, stress, and depression, and it took a toll on our marriage. Over breakfast our counselor, Gary, mentioned the five stages of grief: denial, anger, bargaining, depression, and acceptance (developed by psychiatrist Elisabeth Kübler-Ross).

When Gary defined grief, he named what I hadn't yet been able to, and it was as if the light came on and illuminated an entire room of clutter. Although I hadn't seen it, I had been feeling it—crowding my soul. Up until that point, I honestly couldn't understand why I was angry, why I was not able to talk about it (denial), or why I was struggling to accept that this was happening. I didn't understand that I was grieving. I had to learn that divorce is a death, and that death affects the entire family. In that season I lost two grandparents, a cousin, my beloved childhood home (that was my residence at the time), relationships, and security. I grieved people, places, and even ideals.

Grief can be especially hard to identify when it's attached to good things. A move to a new city or even overseas to a new country is exciting, but you're likely leaving behind friends, family, and familiarity. A new job is wonderful, but perhaps you're grieving a position or role you previously held. Having a baby is joyous and magical, but grieving autonomy of your time (and sleep) is normal. Beginnings, even the ones we initiate and want, are always connected to some form of an ending that we need to acknowledge and process.

Are you experiencing loss? Could you be grieving?
Are you struggling to let go of someone or something?

Trauma: Large T and Small t

I was surprised to learn that trauma is far more common than I had expected. Most of us are familiar with trauma in what some refer to as "large 'T' trauma," but trauma can be overlooked or rationalized as a common experience. *Psychology Today* defines both forms as such: "A large-T trauma is distinguished as an extraordinary and significant event that leaves the individual feeling powerless and possessing little control in their environment."[12] This could bring to mind catastrophic events, war, a car crash, sexual abuse, or bodily injury. "Small 't' traumas are events that exceed our capacity to cope and cause a disruption in emotional functioning."[13] A depiction of this could be infidelity, divorce, legal or financial trouble, a sudden move, conflict or estrangement with family. The effect of trauma can range from affecting one's emotional functioning to posttraumatic stress disorder (PTSD).

There is often a reason why people are on edge, suspicious, hypervigilant, nervous, and afraid. Even when there is no longer a threat of immediate danger, a person recovering from trauma continues to be in a state of heightened alert. We'll explore this later as we're unpacking.

Have you experienced something in your life that you can't seem to get over? Does your body react to certain memories or current experiences that trigger thoughts or images of a past experience?

Do you have a hyperactive nervous system (always on guard and assessing potential danger)?

Depression: Sadness and Melancholy

Staggering statistics from the World Health Organization state that more than 264 million people suffer from depression globally.[14] And it should be noted that this number was reported prior to the COVID pandemic. No doubt this number has increased exponentially.

Perhaps you have asked yourself questions like these:

"Am I just sad?"
"Could this be hormonal?"
"Is this situational?"
"Could it be physical—does this have to do with my brain chemistry and genetics?"
"Maybe I'm just in a melancholy mood?"

Depression can be confusing. I walk on the pensive side of life and have done so since my youth. I'm often reflecting or in deep thought. As an Enneagram Four, I'm drawn to melancholy music, poetry, and art. I completely get what Victor Hugo, author of *Les Misérables*, said: "Melancholy is the happiness of being sad."[15] Over the years, well-meaning people have mistaken my melancholy moments for sadness or depression. I can tell you there is a difference.

Psychology Today helps differentiate, clarifying that "sadness is a normal human emotion, that is usually triggered by a difficult, hurtful, challenging, or disappointing event, experience, or situation. In other words, we tend to feel sad *about something*." Depression, however, is "an *abnormal* emotional state, a mental illness that affects our thinking, emotions, perceptions, and behaviors in pervasive and chronic ways."[16] *Chronic* is always the key word to pay attention to. Feeling sad is human. Living in a chronic state of sadness is living in survival mode.

I once heard depression described as being under a heavy, wet blanket. *Have you experienced that sensation?* I have. There have been times, battling depression, that I have had the capacity to function, albeit slowly and with little to no energy, like a robot whose battery is about to die. And there have also been times when I was so utterly weighed down that I could not get out of bed. The wet blanket was just too wet, just too heavy.

Depression is the strange sensation of feeling things so deeply and feeling numb all at the same time. It's seeing everyone else living in color while you're frozen in black-and-white static. It's as if loneliness swallows you whole. You long for someone to call out to you, and when they do, you don't know whether to rejoice or retract back into yourself. You want to explain what is going on inside of you but struggle to. It's not that you don't have words, it's that you have no way of putting them together. Even with a nuanced description, no one could possibly understand what is going on inside of you, because you don't understand it yourself. It's knowing the right things to do but your body refusing to comply. Or your body does move—on autopilot, like a machine—while you feel completely numb inside, as if nobody is home. Sometimes you get to a point where crying feels hopeful, because then you are feeling something. For me, as a Christian, depression has always been accompanied by great shame.

It's been helpful to understand that experiencing depression need not define me as a depressive, Eeyore-esque person (I'm more like Piglet who has Eeyore days). If you feel you may be experiencing depression—that it's more than melancholy or sadness—there is help. I understand it's hard to take that first step and talk to someone. I didn't want to either. When I finally did, I found that talking to a counselor helped me understand situational depression versus major depressive disorder. Talking with doctors helped me understand *my* physical makeup and how chemical imbalances and hormones can be major factors in mood and energy levels. Don't be afraid to talk to someone. You'll find it's like a super boost to have an expert help you observe.

> Depression is the strange sensation of feeling things so deeply and feeling numb all at the same time.

Do you feel emotionless, overly emotional, or both?

Are you experiencing a sadness you can't seem to shake?

Do you ever ignore a desire or nudge to speak with a counselor or doctor?

Shame: Self-Pity and Perfectionism

Now I'm going to ask you to enter a room you may not want to. But it's one that every human on this planet has entered as well. Shame is a nasty clutter that every human experiences. Brené Brown has given us a gold mine of research on shame; in her best-selling book *Daring Greatly* Brené says, "Shame is the intensely painful feeling or experience of believing that we are flawed and therefore unworthy of love and belonging."[17]

I came to a greater understanding of shame after reading how author and psychotherapist James Burgo breaks down shame into four types:

1. Unrequited love: this includes rejection and unreciprocated love.
2. Unwanted exposure: Burgo gives the example of being called out in public for a mistake or being humiliated by someone walking in on you naked.
3. Disappointed expectation: setting out to do something and failing.
4. Exclusion: being left out.[18]

Does seeing these types of shame bring up hurtful or humiliating memories?

After reading these, I became far more aware of shame and realized that I wasn't labeling it as such. Could shame be cluttering your soul?

In my clearing out and creating space, I've uncovered a good deal of self-pity and perfectionism, which I believe are both by-products of shame. *Self-pity* is the result of paralyzing yourself with shame. *Perfectionism* is trying to work your way out of shame. One gives the perception of being lazy and the other as hardworking. Neither are quite as they seem, and I don't believe them to be mutually exclusive.

I have teetered between the two my entire life. Who wants to admit they struggle with self-pity? I don't, but I will. For me, rejection is a core wound, and I now understand it to be a form of shame. This means that experiencing a normal, everyday form of rejection (extending an invitation or business proposal and being met with a no) can spiral me into self-pity. The pattern looks like wallowing, rejecting yourself for the gross wallowing, and then drumming up the motivation to try again—with no allowance for anything but perfection.

> Perfectionism can never be maintained because it can't be met.

However, perfectionism can never be maintained because it can't be met. This realization—by way of your unmet expectations—sends you back into a bout of self-pity. I see the connection and clutter of all three in my life, and I'm actively working to keep this clutter to a minimum. We can do it as we observe, own, and overcome the shame that's taking up space, and replace it with room to breathe.

Do you recognize shame in your life?
Do you deal with self-pity or perfectionism?

Unforgiveness: Bitterness, Resentment, Hurt, Offense

Now let's go down into the crawl space of our souls. Clutter festers and burrows into the deepest places of the heart and soul looking for a home. Hurt and offense are a daily part of life, but how we respond, what we do with our hurt, is our choice. Like stress, I find there is both everyday hurt, easy enough to let go of, and the sort of hurt that is monumental. Oh, it happens in the everyday, but this is the kind that carries over into every day forward. Actions, words, instances (or lack thereof) that are egregious and unforgettable. Hurt so tender you coddle it like a baby, not realizing that, like a baby, you are nursing it to grow.

Who has wounded you so deeply that not a day goes by that the person is not in your thoughts?

What has been done to you that has hurt you so badly that you believed you might not recover?

We know the importance of forgiveness from a spiritual perspective, but it's also astounding to regard the physical and psychological benefits of forgiveness. Research shows that forgiveness helps release toxic anger, boosts the immune system, and can help rebuild self-esteem. It also is a major stress reliever. Loren Toussaint, a professor of psychology at Luther College, says, "Forgiveness allows you to let go of the chronic interpersonal stressors that cause us undue burden."[19] *How much of our clutter is undue, I wonder?*

One of the quickest ways to create space in your soul is to forgive. Some of us have constructed a fortress around our heart and soul that, with one prayer, can be torn down. Some of us, by holding tight to our hurt, are harboring other people within our very own person. How crowded our souls are.

Forgiveness is not letting someone off the hook, nor does it require reconciliation (and it shouldn't in particular instances, such as abuse). Forgiveness is not for the soul of the offender—it is for you.

And sometimes the person we need to forgive most is ourself.

Taking inventory, naming our clutter, facing what we've been afraid to face, acknowledging that we need help—this is holy work. Remember you are not alone in your observing. The Holy Spirit is *your* wonderful counselor, leading you into truth.

Upon observing, it's easy to become overwhelmed, but be encouraged—you are making progress and already overcoming!

It turns out my grandma did send me the right book. She could see what I hadn't yet observed: I was a woman with severely damaged emotions. She cracked the door and turned the light on. I believe the light is now turned on for you. And now that the doors are opened and you know what you are facing, your eyes are opening up to new life and hope. This is the very purpose of uncluttering our souls—to overcome. To release the identity of victim and walk boldly in our identity as victors in Christ.*

CREATE SPACE

Meditate

Search me, God, and know my heart;
    test me and know my anxious thoughts.
See if there is any offensive way in me,
    and lead me in the way everlasting.
—Psalm 139:23–24 NIV

Reflect

1. Do you recognize any clutter listed above in your own life?
2. Which clutter is taking up the most space?
3. Is there anyone you need to forgive? Do you need to forgive yourself?

Act

Inventory your own clutter with a "Take Note" template available at
trinamcneilly.com/takenote

---

   * Please remember that I am not a professional and this information is not intended to diagnose but rather to inform. As with anything that is chronic or could potentially be an illness, I recommend talking with a qualified and licensed professional.

4

PAY ATTENTION TO YOUR BODY

*Never be so focused on what you're looking for that
you overlook the thing you actually find.*
—Ann Patchett[1]

I love old homes. I'm always drawn to them. The character, the drama, the history. The possibility they possess in a different way than a new build does. Often when referring to older homes, people say, "That house has such good bones." It's true that older homes do have beautiful bones, but more times than not they are in need of repair. Sometimes the work needed is evident, like updating an outdated kitchen or bathroom. Other times, to the naked eye things may appear intact, beautiful in fact, until you hear the floors creak, the faucets hiss, and the windows rattle. These sounds are signals. The house is speaking; it's showing where it needs extra attention and care.

Our bodies, the home to our soul, our living homes, are no different. They, too, creak, rattle, speak, and cry out for care.

At the beginning of my journey, I didn't understand that our bodies will tell us what we cannot, or are unwilling to, tell ourselves. That they will not allow us to keep carrying on. If we don't pay attention to what is happening in our hearts and souls, our living homes will let us know—often in a very uncomfortable way. Pushing through and carrying on doesn't work forever.

It hadn't been a good day. We had attended the funeral of a dear woman whose son has been in our youth group. But Jai hasn't just been a kid in the youth group; through the years Jai has become part of our family. He's become a son and brother. His mother was too young to die, and he was too young to lose his mom.

On a cold winter's day we celebrated Chenita's life, and in doing so we saw many people we hadn't seen in years. Even though I could name the emotion that fit the scenario, sadness and overwhelm, it was one of those days where emotion was vibrating in every frequency possible, yet was still undetectable while you're in the fizziness of it.

Before we left the suburbs, we had a surprise dinner with old friends who were visiting from Florida. We hadn't seen Trent and Keisha for years, and as we caught up, recounting old memories and trading parenting stories, we swung to the other end of the spectrum roaring in laughter. Besides the emotion from the day, my nerves were already supercharged from my personal family issues.

Finally we were home, and I felt so happy to be tucked in my bed, watching an episode of *The King of Queens* to unwind. Then, after the glow of the TV and a mental break from reality dissipated, it was dark. Falling asleep has never come easy for me. Stephen, on the other hand, fell asleep immediately, because he is one of those annoying people who does so every night. There I was alone. Quiet (as much as I treasure it) always invites my mind to work and spin webs of both wonder and worry. If Stephen would have sat up and listened, I would not have even known exactly what to say. There were so many words and, yet, no words. Sometimes I feel like I'm swimming, nearly drowning in thoughts, and yet I can't transform those thoughts to spoken words. It's as if my inner world is in English, but to communicate to the outside I must speak in French. I know only a few words and phrases in French. A busy inner life, I've found, can sometimes make for a lonely life on the exterior. I felt so alone. And cold.

Before I knew it, my body got involved. I couldn't understand why I was so cold. My body began to shiver. It was February; maybe that was why I just could not get warm? We had been outside for some time at the gravesite, after all. My mind scanned all possibilities as to why my teeth were now chattering. I willed myself to stop shaking. *Stop it! Ttt-rrrr-eee-nnn-aaa!*

I called out to God. I prayed a chattering prayer for peace. I imagined Jesus sitting with me—His face so kind. Still I could not stop shivering. Suddenly the shivering turned to shaking and the shaking to a tremor. My arms felt hot and prickly, like I was being poked and prodded with pins and needles. Finally I woke up Stephen to tell him something was wrong with me and that I was scared. He got me more blankets, but I could not stop the trembling. My jaw locked and then panic ensued. I thought my throat might be closing up.

No words of consolation would do. I blurted out that I needed to go to the hospital. Stephen is calm and steady and always one to wait things out, but he could see something was amiss and that I wasn't just spiraling; I was near convulsing. He appeased me, and we called my mom to stay with the kids.

We arrived at the hospital and went through the normal procedures. The nurse brought warm blankets, drew blood, and said they would give me "something" through the IV to help. By the time the doctor arrived, the tremors had subsided. He asked me questions (probably about stress in my life, which I likely denied, because that is what you do when you are in denial), checked my vitals, and read the results of my blood work. Everything was normal. "I think you are experiencing anxiety," he said.

"Anxiety?" Well, that didn't sound very professional coming from a medical doctor. A counselor or psychologist, maybe. Heck, I could have diagnosed anxiety (that I was not in denial about). But this physical business surely had to be something else. Something was wrong with me (not that I wanted anything to be wrong). He gave me another dose of Ativan for the anxiety, and I was, indeed, relaxed when I left, but I was also embarrassed. Embarrassed and confused that my body had acted out like that because of . . . anxiety. It took me a while after that episode to realize that what I had experienced that night was, in fact, a panic attack.

After that episode, I believed that it was noble to keep going. But my body disagreed. Then came the headaches.

I didn't listen to the headaches because I'd always been a headache-y person. Only now they weren't on and off, they were chronic. When it became unbearable, I ended up at the ENT because my ears and jaw were also hurting. The doctor wanted to do a scan, but my insurance wouldn't pay for it—until I did a round of antibiotics. "You *may* have a sinus infection, so take these antibiotics and then come back for a scan," the doctor said. I didn't think I had a sinus infection, but I went home and took the medicine because I am a rule follower and the doctor said to. Within a day, I started feeling ill. My body was saying something else. I figured this particular antibiotic might be harsh on the stomach. I called the nurse, and she told me to power through and keep taking the medicine (which I did not need). And against my better judgment, I did what she said (sometimes following the rules can actually get you in trouble, it turns out).

Signal on top of signal; I was missing an urgent message. The next thing I knew I was breaking out in hives all over my body. I didn't even know they were hives because my entire body was red, and I had swelling patches. Anxiety kicked in and I began to feel dreadfully sick. I ended up going to—you guessed it—the ER.

This time my mom took me. As we sat in a room with the pre-check nurse, answering all the questions and getting my vitals taken, a monitor began to beep. "*Beeeeep. Beeeeep. Beeeeep.*" And as the monitor kept bleating, I began to shake—and chatter—and cry. "I don't want to bbbbb-ee he-rrrr-e." My mom was confused and unsure of what had triggered my sudden reaction. I was confused at my reaction; but I knew what it was. Another thing my body was trying to tell me—that I did not want to hear. The beep of the monitor was the tune of a loved one's two-week stint in the ICU, at the very same hospital I was now at. It hadn't even occurred to my brain; but my body knew—it remembered. My brain caught up and I whimpered, "This hospital! I don't want to bbbb-e here."

Later I learned from my counselor that we carry trauma in our bodies. Those two very long weeks that my loved one was in the ICU were immensely stressful. Many other factors were at play beyond their health, which turned that event into a passage of time that affected the very fibers of my being. I came to understand that it wasn't merely a stressful event; it was a traumatic affair. I wouldn't have labeled it as such. In fact, I didn't; my body did. Every time I've visited that hospital or spoken about that particular situation with my counselor, my body has a physical reaction (it remembers).

The ER sent me home, and I did not get better. This wasn't over. At the counsel of a family friend who is a doctor, I returned again to the ER (at a different hospital), but this time they made my mom leave, and when she did, they began to berate me with questions about drug use or the possibility of eating wild mushrooms. I was so confused, but it turned out that the antibiotic was affecting my liver and they couldn't quite make sense of it.

In a short time I turned jaundice and became so weak that I could barely stand up for ten minutes at a time. I was frightened. After seeing a specialist at the University of Madison, there was nothing I could do but wait it out, pray, and have my liver enzymes monitored every other day. Every time I went to have my blood drawn (at the hospital) and waited for the results, I'd speak Psalm 112:7: "They will have no fear of bad news; their hearts are steadfast, trusting in the LORD" (NIV).

Praise God, eventually I received the news that my liver enzymes were back in a healthy range. I believe God healed me. Recovery, however, took time; it took nearly six months to get my strength and full energy levels back. I'm grateful for our doctor friend who knew exactly what to do. Without his wisdom and God's healing, I could have had a very different outcome.

Through this ordeal I started hearing the insistent voice of my body trying to tell me that all was not well. What could your body be telling you? We are all vastly unique, and how our bodies react to stress, anxiety, fear, and pain (and all other types of soul clutter) can differ. As I've shared, my body reacts in stomachaches, tension headaches, and hives. I've learned this over time by observing—by paying attention to patterns. My goal now is to mitigate the response, lest it become chronic, by paying attention to stressors and anxiety triggers. However, when we miss the cues, our bodies will nudge us. And if we miss the nudge? Our bodies will scream!

Remember, we can't eliminate stress altogether. It's a normal part of our everyday life; it's our body's reaction to pressure and demands. But we can pursue peace and equanimity. It begins with observing. Your body may be speaking to you in what feels like code, and observing these cues and cries will help you figure out what is needed.

For instance, when I get hives, my mind has a tendency to run wild as it remembers the liver injury. However, from paying attention, my mind also now remembers that I get itchy and hives appear on my skin when I'm under considerable stress. Hives mean I need to take care of myself and better deal with stress.

> We can't eliminate stress altogether. . . . But we can pursue peace and equanimity.

My stomach hurts when I'm nervous or anxious about flying. There's a direct connection. I get tension headaches when I'm overwhelmed (which happens whenever I take four children into Target—without fail. "No you cannot have that or that or that!" "Stop running!" "Stop hanging on the cart!" "Get out from under the underwear rack!").

Once we observe what is happening, we can begin to pay attention to when and why it's happening. When we know when and why it's happening, we can take considered action.

Those heart palpitations? Perhaps it's anxiety. Physical exhaustion and loss of appetite may be a signal of depression. The breakouts. The muscle aches. The brain fog. The jaw pain. The upset stomach. They are trying to tell you something.

One of the best ways to listen is to journal or log general observations, to track when your body speaks. Note when you have a headache and what you were doing prior to the pain. For instance, when I began tracking my headaches, I often noticed that too much screen time and scrolling was involved. Movement can also help us feel what we might be missing or have grown used to. Movement releases stagnant energy in our bodies and brings circulation to the areas where we need it. Stretching is a simple and dynamic way to help ease stress and tension in the body, while informing us of what area needs extra attention. Remind your soul of patterns in your body. Remember in your spirit how God has been faithful to you in the past.

With the attention you're giving to the creaks, rattles, and cries of your living home, you're on your way to building a stronger body and spacious soul.

CREATE SPACE

Meditate

Beloved, I pray that you may prosper in every way and [that your body] may keep well, even as [I know] your soul keeps well and prospers.

—3 JOHN 1:2 AMPC

Reflect

1. How is your body speaking? Take time to observe how your body reacts. What is your baseline? What does it feel like when you are worked up or overwhelmed?
2. What could your body be trying to tell you?
3. What helps your body to relax and recover in times of tension?

Observe

Act

Take three minutes to put on calming music (perhaps praise or peaceful piano music). Find a comfortable seated position. Close your eyes. Envision yourself whole: body, soul, and spirit. Breathe deeply and imagine your body strong. Picture your soul spacious and unencumbered. See your spirit regenerated and free.

5

KNOW YOUR (EMOTIONAL) AGE

Most people don't grow up. Most people age. They find parking spaces, honor their credit cards, get married, have children, and call that maturity. What that is, is aging.

—Maya Angelou[1]

L et's just get this out in the open. I'm going to admit something that I'm not proud of (my parents always told me to be careful what I put in writing, and somehow I've been putting far too much in writing ever since). However, it's something that I've observed in myself. Something that forced my attention, really.

Here goes: I am the epic meltdown type (in the privacy of my own home, of course).

When I was a teenager, it wasn't beyond me to, occasionally, lie on the kitchen floor and cry, like a little kid who didn't get their way. I'd feel overwhelmed and it's almost like I'd become overwhelm personified. Those memories are fuzzy to me, and I'd rather not remember. However, there are people who do remember and there is a photo to prove it. My cousin once said, "Trina, you're so dramatic!" I remember piping back, "No, I'm not!" with my trademark eye roll and probably a stomp to prove her wrong.

And then I grew up.

Kind of.

It's easy to believe you are grown up when you reach a certain age and begin to pay bills, hold a job, get married, and have children of your own. However, now that I am a grown-up, I ascertain that age is no indication of maturity. Emotional maturity has nothing to do with chronological age.

I did not come to this conclusion when I reached a certain number of years. I came to it by way of a meltdown. Not mine this time—my daughter's. Children are an excellent mirror.

Ella and I are very different and very much the same. We are both emotional Enneagram Four Types. And she is—surprise—dramatic! Watching her grow up has gifted me the ability to learn a lot about myself that I did not, could not, see in my younger years. Ella has taught me that dramatic is not bad. Dramatic is passionate, lively, expressive, artistic, colorful, and, yes, entertaining. Like me, when Ella becomes overwhelmed, her emotions become larger than life and cloud up every inch of logic. However, when emotions are in check, Ella and I are quite logical, commonsense kind of gals. In elementary school her dramatic personality was evident among her peers. It was cute. It was impressive. It was extra (at times I really thought,

> Emotional maturity has nothing to do with chronological age.

with her singing talent, that "this girl might be famous one day!"). Her little kid meltdowns were just that—little kid meltdowns.

But then one day, when she became a teenager and was having a not-so-little meltdown—emotions whirring like the engines of a jet plane—I tried to calmly talk her down (even as my emotions began to whirr). I gave logic. I validated. I offered help. I shared options. All the while she was spiraling, spinning, panicking.

She ended up on *the kitchen floor.*

I stood, openmouthed, in a stupor.

Not at Ella.

Of course I was watching her—the intense show—but it was as if I was looking beyond her and back at myself.

"Mirror, Mirror of my child: Is this how I, still, react and respond to overwhelm and things not going my way or according to plan?"

It was a crystal clear reflection of me. Suddenly I knew something I had never known before.

My emotional age was that of a teenager.

I had never learned to regulate my emotions.

In that moment I felt shame. I felt disappointed in myself. I felt ill equipped. Below the surface? I felt a tinge of hope and a faint taste of freedom. *Now* I knew the work that needed to be done and I had the motivation to get going with it.

It's not that I hadn't known that I could be overly emotional and go from zero to sixty in 0.2 seconds. It's not that I didn't understand that that was a problem. What I didn't understand was that the root of meltdowns was a lack of emotional maturity and an inability to regulate my emotions. I didn't like losing control of my emotions (who does?!) or letting overwhelm incapacitate me, but I had always felt powerless.

When we feel powerless, we act powerless and perpetuate inaction or unhealthy actions. Now I can see and understand that

---

When we feel
powerless, we act
powerless and
perpetuate inaction
or unhealthy actions.

I wasn't powerless (in Christ we are never powerless). I was simply unaware. Other people may have tried to point my behavior out to me, but I couldn't see until I saw with my own eyes. I didn't need one more ounce of scolding or shaming. What I needed was parenting.

Ella did not need scolding and shaming; she needed parenting and a revelation that she is not powerless to regulate her emotions.

Some of us were given practical tools and guidance to mature into interdependent functioning adults. And the rest of us? Our parents did the best they knew how and then we winged it. This seemingly works, until it doesn't.

Emotional immaturity, I've learned, will affect all relationships.

Your marriage.

Your parenting.

Your friendships.

Your familial interactions.

Your work life.

Your inner life.

Perhaps your parents didn't teach you to regulate your emotions because they were never taught to regulate theirs. Maybe you experienced their meltdowns and outbursts on a regular basis? Is it possible that you learned to retreat during stressful situations? It could be that your parents were model parents, but they didn't discuss how to handle life's challenges and disappointments. To my recollection, not many people were talking about emotional health in the twentieth century.

If we look to how our family of origin deals with stress and overwhelm, as well as how our children are beginning to react to it, this is a great indicator of how we are currently dealing with it. Some of this clutter may have been passed down.

Certainly I have had a plethora of meltdowns since the 1990s, albeit a more muted version of my bright-eyed adolescent variety. The meltdowns of my recent adult years have been steeped in pain and what has often felt like disregard. Many have, indeed, included the floor—the bathroom or closet floor to be exact. At some point I stopped crying out in the kitchen and began retreating to my closet.

Pain has a way of muting passion, while disregard sounds a silent alarm, which warns that it is safer to withdraw and hide than to be seen. When I recall my closet and bathroom moments, the common denominator is that I was so overcome with emotional pain that I could not stand on my own two feet. I couldn't stand out in the open or in the privacy of my closed-in closet. There was nothing left for me to exert; I could only curl up and cry out to God. I know that I am not alone, that many of you have experienced a deluge of pain that brings you lower than your knees.

One day my sister, and, not long after, my mom, brought to my attention that my grandma used to retreat to her room. "Trina, you know Grandma used to always go to her room." I wish I could ask her about her propensity to retreat; I can't. But what I am certain of, because she told me, was that she was drowning in emotional pain. Her wounding was so deep that she could not bear an ounce of tension, disregard, disrespect, insult, or injury, and so I surmise she'd retreat.

As therapist Christine Langley-Obaugh says, "We repeat what we don't repair."[2] I repeat and replicate the behaviors, reactions, and responses of my parents and grandparents, and my children will be prone to repeat mine.

It's funny that, like my grandma, I began to retreat without ever having seen her do so. I share many of her mannerisms that I could not have picked up by association because we lived several states apart. Yet, if I observe the common denominators, I see personality, generational pain, similar wounding, similar sensitivity, and the same genes. Observing family traits and behaviors can serve a great purpose in our progress.

Acting out no longer seemed to be working for me when I was overwhelmed, and thus I began to try my hand at withdrawing. It got so bad that at times I would get up from the dinner table, leaving the room midconversation, to retreat to the safety of my closet. I think it confused my husband and children because I had always been a fighter, always one to speak my piece. But when I felt like I wasn't being heard, I went quiet.

In the closet it would begin with a pity party and then a good long cry. I'd empty my soul and sit in stillness, and in that stillness the Lord would deal with me. In a most loving way, He would parent me. In the stillness and quiet, He would give me a clear view of the clutter. It was never about the clutter of the person that wounded me; it was always about my own soul clutter. My hurt. My response. My choice to heal and grow or to stay imprisoned and become bitter and angry.

When you begin this uncluttering process, to do the hard work of changing twenty-five years' worth of behavioral patterns, you miraculously discover compassion for others and their struggles— and if you do the work, compassion for yourself. The good news is that awareness and compassion move us to action.

Do you find yourself reverting to the behaviors of a certain age when facing a trying moment? When wounded and disregarded, I have a tendency to act like a sulking teenager. This is the age and stage I found myself stuck in. I know adults that respond and react like a toddler when they are overwhelmed by emotions, stress, or life in general. I imagine you do too. It's easy to judge, until you take the speck out of your own eye and take a good look in the mirror.

But as you look in the mirror, don't judge yourself either. Rather, look into the mirror and observe the eyes looking back at you—your very own. *Can you find compassion for yourself?*

Once I get past the signs of aging on my face and look into my own eyes, I always see the passionate, bright-eyed girl I was created to be. She's still there. *Can you see the person you were created to be?*

We are doing the inner work, the unlayering, and the uncluttering, to get to *that* person. That's the person (the soul) that the Holy Spirit will parent into a powerful son or daughter of God.

Let's grow up together.

CREATE SPACE

Meditate

And because you [really] are [His] sons, God has sent the Spirit of His Son into our hearts, crying out, "Abba! Father!" Therefore you are no longer a slave (bond-servant), but a son; and if a son, then also an heir through [the gracious act of] God [through Christ].

—GALATIANS 4:6–7 AMP

Reflect

1. What repeated response(s) do you have to stress, overwhelm, or pain?
2. What is your emotional age? Think of the different stages of

Observe

> a person (baby, toddler, child, teenager, young adult, mature adult) and the typical behaviors of each stage. Which best matches your emotional responses?
>
> 3. Are you repeating behaviors or responses? Do you mirror anyone in your family of origin?

Act

Pray this prayer:

Father of Lights, I give You permission to search and sort through all my soul clutter—whether I've tucked it away or find myself tripping over it daily. Reveal what I cannot see and what I might be repeating. Help me to observe without judgment. Help me to observe with anticipation and expectation of growth and emotional and spiritual health. I ask You today to parent me. Teach me what I have not yet learned. Give me the grace to not rear up, run away, or retreat. Rather, Holy Spirit, help me to stand up and grow up into the son/daughter You are calling me to be so that I may participate in Your kingdom. Thank You for sending the Spirit of Your Son into my heart that cries out: Abba, Father. I no longer identify as a slave to sin or my past way of living; I recognize that I am a son/daughter and, therefore, an heir. In Jesus' name, amen.

6

SAY GOODBYE TO

COMFY CLUTTER

———————

We comfort ourselves by reliving memories of protection.

—Gaston Bachelard[1]

I t was so strange moving back to my childhood home as an adult—as a parent myself. Initially, I resisted the move because it felt like going back—in every sense of the word. My parents had found a new home and our beloved family home, tucked between trees on the cul-de-sac, had been without people for a good six months. My father asked Stephen and me if we might be interested in buying the house and moving back to town. "No way!" I said.

Moving back to my hometown would be weird enough; moving back into my childhood home was just too much. Also, I thought it was a stretch for us financially. I was in my own stage of stretching, bloated and ready to pop with our second child, Luke. (Like to the point that a stranger stopped me in Walgreens to ask if I was pregnant with twins. Thank you for your concern, sir, but that would be a no, and I still have three months to go.)

Between the assuredness of my father and husband, it felt like my opinion didn't matter (at least that is what I believed back then, which meant I responded accordingly). "Trina doesn't like change"—they both knew this. And they weren't wrong. I had a hard enough time leaving home the first time around. But I went along with buying my childhood home because I didn't have a great counter argument, I was slightly interested, and I had absolutely zero energy for a fight. Also, no one in my family (including myself) was ready to say goodbye to that grandpa-person-of-a-home. So my family moved (I waddled) in.

Settling my daughter into my and my sister's old room, my newborn son into my brother's room, and myself and Stephen into my parents' room was peculiar. Yet, in no time at all, I was comfortable. Comfortable hemmed within the walls that held my stories, my memories, and my history. The soul of that home had always been rest and retreat, and even with my young, energetic family the home still emanated those peaceful qualities. And in time I found I enjoyed the process of making the home "ours."

Familiar, it turned out, was cozy. Familiar, it turns out—even when it's not in our best interest—is comfortable.

About five years into living in my childhood home—five years of undecorating, decorating, having babies, buying businesses, attending my home church, and my kids going to the school I graduated from—everything began to break apart at the seams. The things I never imagined would change, changed.

I had no idea how to sort the mental and emotional overload and process pain in a home that was like a museum of memories. Growing up, I had strong influences in my life (some personalities were larger than life) that, in one way or another, ingrained in me that "everything would be okay." Everything will be okay, because I'll take care of you. Everything will be okay if you follow these rules. Everything will be okay if you have enough faith. Everything will be okay if you follow this system. Trust me. Trust God. Trust how it's always been. Trust the plan.

Suddenly, everything was not okay.

Following the rules and formulas didn't add up. Obedience and a strong faith did not circumvent pain. Trust did not equate to security. My identity and security were completely shaken.[*]

Being in that home was a dichotomy of comfort and cruelty. I'd curl up in corners that had held me when I cried as a child and absorbed my tears as a teen. The house knew me. On the other hand, it felt cruel to be in a place that was like a living movie screen. This is where we had all been *together*. We may have been dysfunctional, as most families are, but we weathered the storms *together*. Every day my body felt like it was screaming, *You've got to get out of here*, but also, *You can't leave, this is all you have left of "what was."* This is where your family was together. Where Grandpa sat on the sofa watching the Cubs. Where Grandma sat on the covered patio reading. *See them there?* This living room is where, no matter what, everyone came together for Christmas.

Friends noticed my waning and would tell me, "Trina, I think the best thing for you would be to leave that house." Deep down,

---

[*] I write more in depth about this in my book *La La Lovely*.

I knew the truth. I would, indeed, have to leave my beloved home. However, it was no longer just my childhood home; it was now my children's childhood home. And they loved that grandpa-person-of-a-home just as much as I did. They loved the breeze between the trees, the long hallway they could run up and down, the swing in the living room, and the basement that ignited imagination as well as an inclination to run, as fast as you could, up the stairs just in case someone or something was behind you.

Even when I knew my days there were numbered, when I knew my friends were right, I still told myself that I was comfortable there. I had been telling myself a story for a long time, which went like this: *What if I never feel at home again? The house will miss us. What if my children will be wounded if we leave? They love this home and neighborhood. I'll never have anything as nice as this home again.*

The truth was, I was severely uncomfortable; I was in so much pain, and my body was screaming with a host of issues. Eventually, by the relentless prodding of the Holy Spirit, I began to pay attention to what He was saying. He challenged the stories I had been telling myself with the stories of people past, in the Bible, along with God's Word of hope and expectation:

> *What if, when you leave, you find freedom? What if your children are just fine? In fact, what if they learn adaptability that will serve them later in life? What if they find freedom? What if they learn to not fear change? What if I'm building a home for you that moths cannot destroy and time cannot take from you? What if you truly make your home in Me, Trina? What if I'm doing a new thing? What if I have something better for you? What would your one-day-someday house look like?*

As we become acutely aware of the clutter in our lives, it is easy to assume we would become uncomfortable with that clutter crowding us. But even when we are uncomfortable with our clutter, we have a tendency to resist change and letting go. Whatever the clutter is for you, it's hard to let go of because it's personal, familiar, difficult to dismiss. We can become so accustomed to our clutter that many times we can't see it for what it is anymore. We mistake discomfort for comfort because discomfort is familiar. And when we have but an inkling of our cramped conditions, we convince ourselves that we can manage fine in the tight places—"It's just enough space," we say. We become comfortable in our confinement—in chains. I think of the children of Israel in bondage, enslaved to Egypt. They became comfortable and accustomed to their captivity. They cried out to God for freedom and when He began the process of walking them out of their captivity and oppression, they questioned the process, complained, and even resisted.

Has what oppressed you become part of your identity?

While I applaud the work to remove stigmas concerning mental health issues, along with the progress made in creating space for vulnerability and sharing our stories, I am grieved when I see people take on the identity of the very thing that is causing them to suffer. Have you noticed?

Fear becomes part of our identity. Stress becomes competitive. Anxiety, a label we wear around our neck, like a tribe—when the Bible clearly says be anxious for *nothing* (Philippians 4:6–7). I'm not suggesting that we live in la-la land and deny things such as fear, stress, and anxiety; I'm saying we don't have to live under the identity and bondage of such things.

> We mistake discomfort for comfort because discomfort is familiar.

I've been in bondage to fear, anxiety,

and depression, but in Christ I am free. Although I may be in a season where I am fighting anxiety, the truth is my identity is still that of a victor, not a victim. And I want my life to bear witness to that. This doesn't mean I can't or won't talk about my struggles; it means that *I am not my struggles.* I prove this by not giving more attention, more weight, to my struggles (to the clutter) than I give glory (weight) to God.

God must be exalted above it all.

When we become too comfortable with our clutter, it can almost become a Stockholm syndrome of the soul. Some of us have formed attachments and bonds to our captors. We feel safe in the tight spaces of bondage and captivity, because liberation and freedom are not familiar.

Familiarity isn't comfort that can sustain. In fact, familiarity is, simply, familiarity. Freedom may feel unknown, because it is foreign to you. But it's not to God. Freedom may feel different, but how you feel isn't working for you anyway. We must realize that true comfort can only come from the Comforter. This can feel confusing because the Comforter will prompt us to take action, to do things that are uncomfortable, leading to growth and change. However, we can be assured that He never withholds His comfort as we wade through pain, submit to the process of change, and conform to the purpose and will of God.

Have you heard this saying by Tony Robbins: "Change happens when the pain of staying the same is greater than the pain of change"?[2] Have you experienced it yet? There will come a point when the comfort of familiarity can no longer sustain you. The comfort of familiarity is not a match for a soul in pain. Eventually the pain will either propel you or paralyze you. Neither are comfortable, yet only one leads to growth and life.

I've made the choice to change. Won't you? It's uncomfortable getting uncomfortable, but that's when you know change is beginning. Change is never comfortable, but I can promise you that living with a soul that is bound and cluttered is far more uncomfortable.

> Eventually the pain will either propel you or paralyze you. Neither are comfortable, yet only one leads to growth and life.

It wasn't easy leaving my home. I had to comb through physical clutter while sorting through my mental and emotional clutter at the same time. As I went through the process of letting go, I found that I was never alone. The Holy Spirit was leading me in this space-making process. And with His help I was beginning to get a glimpse of a new dawn. You're not alone either, and He will be faithful to lead you too. All the things that you need to let go of, you can let them go. Wide-open spaces await you

CREATE SPACE

Meditate

Some sat in darkness and in the shadow of death,
   prisoners in affliction and in irons.
Then they cried to the LORD in their trouble,
   and he delivered them from their distress.
He brought them out of darkness and the shadow of
   death,
   and burst their bonds apart.
   —Psalm 107:10, 13–14 ESV

Reflect

1. Have you mistaken familiarity for comfort? What familiar things, places, or people have you sought comfort in?
2. Are there certain types of soul clutter that have become your identity? Name them, surrender them, and ask God to help you live in the identity of the victorious daughter/son that you are.
3. Have you been praying for freedom yet resisting the process that God is trying to walk you through? Get honest. Is your pain propelling or paralyzing you?

Act

Create a vision board (or Pinterest board) of what change you anticipate and what your clutter-free future *could* look like. For me, I wanted to visualize a future home, so I created a "One-Day-Someday House" board on Pinterest.* I wasn't anywhere near being able to make a home like the photos I was pinning, but the Holy Spirit was expanding my heart to trust by dreaming. Your vision board may have nothing to do with home. Consider where your heart and soul need expansion. Could you find imagery to help you envision the change and future you long to see?

---

* You can visit my "One-Day-Someday House" board at: pinterest.com/lalalovelyblog /one-day-some-day-house/.

7

DON'T FORGET THE BOXES
IN THE BASEMENT

———

Someone I loved once gave me a box full of
darkness. It took me years to understand that this
too, was a gift.
                                    —Mary Oliver[1]

I love basements. Our next home will not have a basement and
I feel rather panicky about this. When I was a kid, the basement was anything I dreamed it to be—a store, a house, a roller
rink, a restaurant, a movie theater (when you have long winters, the
basement is the next best thing to being outside). In junior high
I packed up my favorite belongings (my Swatch phone, a poster
of Kirk Cameron, my comforter and pillow), pushed a hide-a-bed

into a storage room—yes, a storage room—and moved into our basement. I was desperate to not share a room with my little sister, who is five years younger.

My parents saw my resilience. *Trina, who was always scared, actually stayed down there all night?!* And so they had a proper room built out for me. My room had a Southwestern-pattern wallpaper border, green carpet, and a waterbed. I was living my best teenage life in that basement, sleeping in until noon with not a peep of sunlight.

These days our basement is mostly for walking on the treadmill and rambunctious children—when they get rowdy, I yell, "Take it to the basement!" Maybe most importantly, basements hold all the things we don't want to get rid of, the things we might "someday" need—old photos, décor we love and might use again, baby clothes we can't part with, family pieces, extra coats, and curated pieces of our past lives.

In my opinion, basements are fun, functional, and fascinating. Or utterly terrifying. Let's be honest, all basements have a bit of a creeper factor (maybe not so much for walk-out basements with big windows), especially if we are talking about an old home with an unfinished basement or a dated one that is piled floor to ceiling with stuff. In my experience the only way to exit a basement is to run up the stairs (two steps at a time), as fast as you can, as if something or someone was behind you, as if your life depended on it.

When we moved my children asked me, "What about the man who lives in the storage room?"

Wait, what?! "There is no man who lives in the storage room!" I definitely told them.

"Well, Uncle J.J. said there is a man who lives behind the furnace" (remember this was Uncle J.J.'s home when he was a kid). No wonder they ran up those basement stairs too.

My grandma Eleanor's basement was *the* basement from

childhood that is seared in my memory. Below her home, on Avenue N on the South Side of Chicago, was a treasure maze of anything and everything. It was a space that creeped me out and made me curious. Every time we'd visit, J.J. and I would try to work up the courage to go exploring in the basement. As soon as we'd open the door and step onto the windy stairs that snapped and creaked, it felt risky. One side of the basement was finished in a 1950s kind of way; there was an exercise bike, a TV, a couch, and a twin bed always covered with stuff. No one ever wanted to watch the TV down there, except maybe my grandpa who was probably hiding from my grandma.

To the right was a door that led into the unfinished part. This part didn't even look like a basement, at least not the ones I was used to. It looked like a cellar—a creepy cellar from a horror movie. There were boxes piled floor to ceiling, shelves of this and that, makeshift racks holding clothes from people past and eras gone by. The space was overflowing with old things, interesting things, and oddities that most would consider rubbish. Items sure to never be taken out or used again. Family pieces either inherited or intended to be passed down, incapable of being trashed. In another corner was a shelf with canned goods, freshly jarred vegetables, and extra grocery items (Grandma Eleanor would have definitely been ready for 2020). And to take the creep factor to the next level, there was a dilapidated dog pen for their deceased German shepherd, Gretchen. Of course, J.J. and I were convinced Gretchen's dog ghost lived in that pen.

The thing about my grandma's basement, my mom's basement, and even my basement, is that you never can really recall *all* that you have packed away. You may remember the important things or items front and center, but there are always those things we forgot that we saved. Things we hold on to. Things we can't let go of. Things we are surprised by when we get to sorting through the stuff. After my grandma died, we finally convinced my grandpa Warren to leave that old house in Hegewisch. This meant my mom, my cousin Nicole, and I spent a week going through all the things my grandma had saved and stored away. Some of it was lovely and meaningful; much of it was junk or completely useless. Unnecessary trifles, bits and bobs taking up space for decades.

I think the same can be true of our souls. We have the obvious front and center clutter, and underneath that is something else entirely.

What Is a Stronghold?

I wonder what is packed deep in the basement of your soul? The boxes at the very bottom.

Inherited mental clutter, maybe? "Well, my grandma was a worrier, my mom is a worrier, and it seems I am too."

Perhaps hurtful memories stuffed away in a safe place? We rationalize that these things shouldn't be a bother because they are out of sight and out of mind. Yet they aren't. Somehow, they will continue to keep turning up in your main living space. This kind of clutter is nothing short of a stronghold, and those cannot be tucked away. They must be acknowledged, named, owned, and torn down.

The term *stronghold* appears more than fifty times in the Bible.[2] It's an interesting term because in the Psalms, David described God as a stronghold for the oppressed, a stronghold in times of trouble (9:9–10, paraphrase mine). In the New Testament we see that we are to pull down strongholds (2 Corinthians 10:4–5).

Interestingly enough, the *Cambridge Dictionary* defines a stronghold in two manners that concur:

1. A building or position that is strongly defended
2. A place or area where a particular belief or activity is common[3]

Is there a certain belief or activity in your life that is common? Perhaps one that was or is common to your grandparents or parents—to the generations?

In all families there are strongholds. I've identified mine, packed away in the basement, passed down, multiplying into an inordinate amount of soul clutter. The way I see it is that I have two choices. I can relent and put up with these strongholds, or I can own them—face them head-on—and overcome them, inviting my children and their children into a new legacy.

As far back as I can remember, worry has been on the main floor of my life. Worry might seem harmless. At times it even feels rather responsible. If I love someone, I worry about him or her. If I really care about a situation, I give it time, attention, and space.

I've had to conclude that there is a false responsibility attached to worry. Thinking about something or someone does not change a situation or that person. It's equivalent to motion versus action. The motion will take you nowhere, but it will wear you down.

Unless we get to sorting and unpacking at a deeper level, we are left with mitigation efforts that fall short.

I had to realize that while worry is present on the main level, it's fear that lurks in the boxes in the basement. It's fear that I have to unpack. It's fear that has been a stronghold in my life.

Joyce Meyer defines a stronghold as "an area where we're stuck in bondage—any part of our lives in which Satan imprisons us. He does this by causing us to think a certain way—a way based on lies we've been told. As long as we believe the lies, we will stay imprisoned by those strongholds." Joyce goes on to say that to enjoy freedom, we have to learn to use God's mighty weapons.[4]

What Do We Do with Boxes?

What do we do with these strongholds—these beliefs that imprison us? These boxes in the basement?

First, we must believe that we are not powerless. God says that the weapons we have been given are mighty (Ephesians 6) and He's *given us the power* to pull down strongholds, cast down arguments, and take captive every thought to the obedience of Christ (2 Corinthians 10:4–5).

Second, we take action to unpack the box and name the lie (belief).

Third, we confess our agreement with that belief (own our part)—this is rightful responsibility. Confess to God and also consider confessing to a friend or trusted person in your life—this is biblical, it brings what was dark into the light, and it gives us accountability and support.

Fourth, we replace the lies with truth. We align our beliefs to truth—God's Word.

We do not have to be stuck in our ways—stuck with the clutter in the basement of our soul. We can change, and it begins with our thinking. In fact, when we change our thinking, we can change our lives. Both the Bible and science give evidence of this.

> **When we change our thinking, we can change our lives.**

Dr. Caroline Leaf, a neuroscientist who was part of initial research on neuroplasticity (the brain's ability to adapt and change) and author of *Switch On Your Brain*, tells us:

Today, there is an increasing body of evidence that the brain changes according to experience. The anatomy and physiology of the human brain is much more malleable and plastic than we once thought—the brain changes according to how we use it!

Dr. Leaf goes on to say,

Our brains can change as we think (neuroplasticity) and grow new brain cells (neurogenesis). Using the incredible power in our minds, we can persist and grow in response to life's challenges. We can take our thoughts captive and change how we think, speak and act! Our brains can create new neural pathways and we do this by renewing our minds.[5]

What might you need to unpack? Where do you need to change your thinking?

Judgmental spirit	Lying
Fear	Jealousy
Pornography	Anger
Worry	Bitterness
Substance abuse	

You have the ability to create new neural pathways. Imagine ones of

Peace	Hope
Contentment	Beauty
Joy	Love

What about when doing this feels a little too overwhelming? Remember, you have a God who is your stronghold—stronger than any hold that sin or a wrong belief may have on you. He is a strong tower that we are told to run into and *we will be saved* (Proverbs 18:10). In studying strongholds, I learned that the Hebrew term *misgav,* which translates to *stronghold*, means a high place of refuge.[6] Are you noticing how our two definitions of *stronghold* are continuing to contrast? Light, dark. High, low. Bondage, security. Further "a stronghold was a fortification of last resort where people sought safety during an enemy attack."[7] When the Enemy attacks, and you can be sure that he will as you work to tear down generational strongholds, get up out of that basement and go to the high place— the stronghold for the oppressed—to the refuge in which you can always find safety.

I am continually amazed at the beautiful detail that God gives to everything. A stronghold for a stronghold.

No matter how dark, don't be afraid of the basement and its boxes. You have the power to turn on the lights, sort through the clutter, and walk boldly back up the stairs with a confidence that no one or nothing is behind you except for Christ.

CREATE SPACE

Meditate

For the weapons of our warfare are not carnal but mighty in God for pulling down strongholds, casting down arguments and every high thing that exalts itself against the knowledge of God, bringing every thought into captivity to the obedience of Christ.
—2 CORINTHIANS 10:4–5 NKJV

Reflect

1. Give yourself a moment to reflect on your life. Think of your parents, your grandparents, and your siblings. Do you see any

similarities? Any patterns in outlooks, behaviors, how you deal or
don't deal with life?

2. Ask the Holy Spirit to show you if there are any strongholds in
your life and to identify them.

3. How has this particular type of clutter, or stronghold, been
affecting your life?

Act

Work on creating new beliefs. Find a truth in God's Word that specifically
counteracts the lie and commit it to memory. When that stronghold tries
to entangle you again, use the mighty weapon of God's Word—the sword
of the Spirit—taking the thought captive by speaking the truth. Not only
are you pulling down the stronghold, you are also creating new neural pathways in your mind (which we know is part of our soul). In my life this hasn't
meant that I never feel afraid; it means when I feel afraid I tell fear it has to
leave because God has given me a spirit of power, love, and a sound mind
(2 Timothy 1:7). Other weapons we can use are prayer, fasting, and worship.

Pray this prayer:

*Lord, I repent for any place that I have given to the Enemy who has
pushed and shoved and worked for a place. Today I knock down this
stronghold. I evict fear and anxiety [name your stronghold here] from
my life—from my soul (mind, will, emotions) and my body. I create
space for Jesus. I am Your place and You are mine.*

8

GO THROUGH TO GET OUT

There is no way out of one's inner life, so one had
better get into it. On the inward and downward
spiritual journey, the only way out is through.
—Parker J. Palmer[1]

H ave you ever read the beloved children's book *We're Going on a Bear Hunt*?[2] It's the simple story of a family who sets out on an adventure to find a bear. During their hunt they encounter several obstacles (tall grass, mud, a forest) that they can't go over or under. Instead, they discover they have to go through.

This story by Michael Rosen came back to me recently. I read this singsong story to Ella and Luke over and over when they were little. My cousin Kristen gave this book to us as a gift. She had read it to her children. Whenever I read the book, I always hear it in her suburban Chicago accent. The last sound of the last word of the last sentence, dragging on and downward.

"We've got to go through itttttttt."

That had taken on a new meaning for me in the thicket of life I'd been facing. I'd been living *through itttttttt* for the past decade. Parents divorcing, deaths, a monumental move, estrangement, trauma, depression, and anxiety—everything we've been talking about so far.

Maybe you've been *through itttttttt*, or you're currently going *through itttttttt*. The thing is, if you've been through some kind of personal hell, there is no such thing as *it* simply coming to an end. Because at the end of *it* there you are. And you are no longer the same person you were before *it*. There is now debris. Residue. Damage. Soul clutter. You may even feel a stranger to your own soul.

I found it surprising that on the other end of a traumatic situation and life-changing event, I hadn't necessarily gone through it—I merely survived it. The true going through often happens after the event itself: the sorting, the processing, the surrender, the forgiving, the acceptance, the growth, the healing. This kind of going through really only happens when we choose to travel into our pain. This means that we have the choice to do the healing work during difficult situations, so long as we choose to travel into the pain, the moment we recognize it as such.

The temptation, however, will always be to run, escape, or expect rescue. At least those are my go-tos.

The first time I tried to run away I was around ten years old. I remember marching into our very blue, very 1980s kitchen to declare to my mom, "I just want you to know that I'm running away!" Eyes closed, nose in the air, I marched back down the long hallway to my room. I suppose I wanted her to beg me to stay. Instead, she brought a suitcase and said, "Here you go; you might need this." I was stunned. I could imagine a mom on TV responding like this, but not my mom. There was no backing down now. I got to packing and then promptly climbed out my window—everyone knows you don't run away walking out of the front door; I wanted to do this right. I made it down the street but never left the cul-de-sac because I was afraid. My mom knew this about me, which is why she gave me the suitcase and sent me packing.

The second time I ran away, I was twelve and had good reason. While my parents were down the street at the neighbors', I had the harebrained idea to back my dad's brand-new car in and out of the driveway. My cousin seconded that this was "like, for sure" totally a great idea. As it turned out, I wasn't so clear on steering when it came to backing up. I got a little too close to my mom's blue Safari minivan, and before I knew it . . . *Screech! Scrape! Scratch!* Obviously, I had to run away.

This time I left the street and made it to the neighborhood park. My cousin again concurred that this was a good idea. She lived across the street from the park and promised to bring me food every day. I made a makeshift home under the slide and hid there until dark. And yet again I was afraid (see the pattern?). In the end, I was more afraid of the dark than my parents' wrath. I rode my ten-speed home and confessed.

You Are the Guardian of Change

Although responsibility usually gets the last word these days, my penchant for running followed me into adulthood.

Down the street, to the park, across the Atlantic, into my closet.

However far I've made it, I've never been able to run away from God. He is a parent, and He has been parenting me *through* my reactive pattern of fixating on escape and running away (I guess I'll just call it what it is: a coping mechanism). He's even called my bluff a few times, once with a "Here's your suitcase!" and off to London I flew.

Whether I've been holed up in my closet or across the pond, I've learned that we can never run away from ourselves (our problems, our pain). As the saying by Jon Kabat-Zinn goes, "Wherever you go, there you are."[3] What isn't always so obvious is that when we fantasize about escape, rescue, and running, we forget that it is, after all, fantasy. We cannot escape our own minds. So far, no matter how hard I've wished and prayed, no person has rescued me from my troubles. I've looked to my father. I've looked to my husband. I've looked to leaders. I've looked to friends. I've looked to books. No one has the power to save us, except Jesus and then ourselves. He is the Savior of our souls, and we are the guardians of our own change.

You are the guardian of your own change. And nothing will (or can) change in you unless *you* make a decision to change. Unless you allow God to reveal and heal. Unless you take action to sort through and go through.

Change is messy and undoubtedly so much work, which we already know. This is why we don't want to get into it. But, Dear Reader, chances are, how you are living is already messy. The lie you are tempted to believe is that not everyone has it as bad as you. Not everyone has as much (or as difficult) work to do to heal. Don't be deceived. We can never fully know what someone has been through, is going through, or is working through—even when we've been given a glimpse into their lives. As much as people spill their stories all over the Internet, it's never the full story. We just can't know. There's always a decade-long memoir of heartbreak and the hard work of going through behind the scenes.

> No one has the power to save us, except Jesus and then ourselves. He is the Savior of our souls, and we are the guardians of our own change.

Change Happens from the Inside Out

This means:

- We cannot know what truly needs changing if we do not pay detailed attention to what is happening within us.
- Things often look worse before they get better.
- People may mistake your inner work for no work at all. This work is about transformation, not transaction. Transformation takes time.
- The inner work of heart transformation and the renewing of the mind yield outer fruit.

Inner work can sound daunting. Especially for those of us who are too much in our heads already. I understand that for a good many of you, the whole idea is to get out of your head. You overthink and underact. Me too. But what I've learned over time, and confirmed in Parker Palmer's book *Let Your Life Speak*, is this: the way out of your head (your mind, will, emotions) is to get into it.

All of the inner work I was doing to sort through the clutter was not futile; it was purposeful. And the length of time that it was taking was no one's business but the Holy Spirit's and mine. As humans we build and review our lives around time—seconds, minutes, hours, days, months, years, but time is irrelevant to God—He does not live within its confines. He is not impatient with you or me. He is measured and thorough. I realized that the process of getting into my inner life was just that, a process. And processes take time.

The soul is not a formula to figure out, nor a problem to solve. It is the psyche and the substance of a human being. Your soul, like your spirit, does not die. It is not a body that decays and returns to dust. It is your essence that will one day return to eternity when your body expires. Whether you realize it or not, your soul is *already* on a journey. We are travelers on this earth. We are traveling through. And only you, Dear Reader, have the ability to change the trajectory. You can ignore, resist, and object, or you can observe, own, and overcome. Which will you choose?

The only way out of a busy mind is to first travel into it. Naturally, our clutter is an obstruction to our view. It can slow movement or threaten an all-out halt. How, then, do we journey into it? One step at a time, sorting one piece at a time (just as you would clothes from your closet: keep, trash, donate), being led through the design of your life by the light of God's love.

Movement is never impossible, but it must be careful and thoughtful.

The Way Through

When my family and I moved away from my childhood home, the one I had been so fruitlessly holding on to, relief wasn't instant. It took time to ease into this change and sort through what had happened. A few months after moving, I crashed. As in couldn't get out of bed except to feed my family, crashed. The adrenaline waned, and I was exhausted mentally, emotionally, and physically. It was summertime, warm and colorful, but for me everything felt cold and dark. My spirit was eager to sort through clutter, but my flesh was weak. I felt like I was stuck, immobile in the muck of depression. I had no solution. I couldn't see my way through. One morning in a phone conversation, my mom read me a passage from Psalms:

> I wait for the LORD, my soul waits,
> and in his word I hope;
> my soul waits for the Lord

more than watchmen for the morning,
more than watchmen for the morning.

O Israel, hope in the LORD!
For with the LORD there is steadfast love,
and *with him is plentiful redemption.*
—Psalm 130:5–7 ESV (emphasis mine)

"God has a thousand ways to set you free," she reminded me. It was easy to believe that He had a thousand ways to set others free. In fact, we had been praying that exact prayer for someone that we both love. Yet I had never thought to pray it for myself. It's easy to have faith and believe for others; it's not as easy to believe for our own freedom and healing. Our vision is obstructed in the smog of our own mind, but God sees from end to beginning and He has a thousand ways.

How quickly we forget. Not only had I forgotten this scripture, I needed to be reminded Jesus is *the* Way. After that conversation I took to my journal and wrote out, in faith, what I wanted to see on the other side of this.

- I would like to see Stephen in a calling and career that he is fulfilled in. I can't see a way, but You are the Way.
- I'd like to see us both in a good community using our gifts, thriving, with godly, growing friendships. I don't see the way, but You are the Way.
- I'd like to know what You would have me continue to do. Write? Speak? Please make a way.
- I'd like to see my children with good friends and great opportunities for their futures—You are the Way.
- I'd like to see myself strong, mentally and emotionally. Happy—full of joy. You are the Way.

- I'd like to see my marriage strong and vibrant—I don't know the way, but You are the Way.
- I'd like to see myself sharing Your Word—spreading hope, encouraging women. As I submit and abide, would You be the Way?

What would you like to see—even if you can't see a way?

We don't need to see the way, because as we are learning, Jesus is *the* Way. We must simply keep our eyes on Jesus. If He is with us—in us—then we already have the way, even if we don't yet see it. It's never been about us having to know the way (God can make any path straight—within the design of your inner life as well as in the outer steps we take to live out our every day).

Two things of note about the way:

1. His way is gentle and humble. We learn His way by joining our life with His (Matthew 11:28–30).
2. He will direct and make our paths straight and plain when we completely trust Him and don't try to figure out everything on our own (Proverbs 3:5–6). Trying to figure everything out is exhausting and just works against us.

Whatever you've come up against:

Depression
Fear
Pain
Anxiety
Discouragement
Unforgiveness

Observe

Chronic Stress
_____ *[name your clutter]*

We can't avoid it.
We've got to go through it.
We're not overwhelmed because Jesus is the Way.

CREATE SPACE

Meditate

"He is wooing you from the jaws of distress
to a spacious place free from restriction,
to the comfort of your table laden with
choice food."
—Job 36:16 NIV

Reflect

1. Do you fantasize about running or escape? Do you notice any patterns in these thoughts?
2. What are you avoiding going through or getting into? Why?
3. Who have you expected to rescue you? Are you willing to accept that only God can rescue and save you, and you are the guardian of your own change?

Act

Make a list of what you desire to see, even if (especially if) you can't see a way. Declare Jesus is the Way after each desire/prayer.

9

PARTICIPATE IN YOUR LIFE

You cannot find peace by avoiding life.
—Virginia Woolf the author *The Hours*

As a child, if I didn't like what someone was saying, I'd put my fingers in my ears and say out loud, "*Lalalalala*, I can't hear you!" in the tone of a robot.

While I grew out of that immature form of avoidance, my propensity to avoid only evolved over my lifetime. In my twenties, when faced with things I didn't like or understand, like finances, I avoided them by passing the responsibility. I had never been great with numbers and believed that Stephen was better with the finances. I offered my administrative skills by saving receipts and scheduling the bills; however, Stephen had to handle the budget—the numbers.

In my thirties I was ready to be a grown-up and take on the things I tended to avoid, but when things got tough, budget formulas seemed inconsequential. Try as I might to face reality, I had no idea what to do with a reality that didn't match up to my ideals. Forget putting my fingers in my ears—I was now more like an ostrich with its head in the sand. At least that is what someone in my life kept telling me. "Get your head out of the sand," they would say.

In life there are things so overwhelming (and it matters not whether they suddenly slam into you or slowly worm their way in) that before you have time to think or process what's happening, your mouth sputters out the likes of:

"I can't handle this."

"I can't deal with this."

"This is too much."

When we don't know how to cope, we cope by not coping; we avoid. Avoidance becomes an option we don't have to decide to take. It's a place we can pretend nothing is happening, and, therefore, we don't have to change.

To the untrained eye, avoidance looks like doing a lot of nothing. I can tell you it's anything but. It takes considerable energy to avoid something or someone, push back against change, overthink your circumstances, or pretend you can't hear or see what's going on when there's actually no avoiding, only delay. I never fully viewed my avoidance as inaction because I was spending almost all my time (other than mothering) introspecting, coping, managing, preparing for every "what if," and planning for "when and then." All of the mental gymnastics required a level of doing, even if just in the mind.

> When we don't know how to cope, we cope by not coping; we avoid.

I think of the energy we exert when we avoid a physical uncluttering in our homes. Because it feels like a daunting project, we convince ourselves that it's easier to tidy around clutter than to organize or get rid of it. Instead of going through our piles we straighten or shift them; we move them from counter to cabinet, floor to floor, room to room. Surely clearing out will take far more time and effort than cleaning up does, we tell ourselves (as we exert more energy with all our emotional laboring over this looming task). In the long run we are exerting more energy because we are repeatedly tidying and cleaning things that we wouldn't have to, if only we'd take the time to go through the process of uncluttering. There would be fewer dishes to wash, fewer clothes to fold, fewer toys to pick up, fewer trinkets to dust around (and likely less guilt and emotional labor).

At my worst, during bouts of depression and extreme over-whelm, I spent an embarrassing amount of time staring at the wall, so vanquished mentally that I couldn't move physically—too over-whelmed to even turn on the TV. The decision of what show to put on was literally too much.

To some this may sound extreme, and others know exactly what this feels like. It feels like something is exceptionally wrong with you. There must be—if the smallest decisions, like what to eat, wear, or watch, are debilitating. It's as though your voice is foreign; it's forgotten how to communicate, or maybe it never knew how to in the first place. It seems everyone and everything are in motion, except you. One unkind word will swallow you whole. You feel as if you've been left behind—even when you are right in the middle of it all. You're flawed, defective even. Trapped in your own clutter. And you feel so much shame for not being able to get out from under it—when other people seem able to just toss it off.

Why couldn't I get moving? Take action? Make a decision? Friends of mine, along with every person I scrolled past on Instagram, were out there hustling, living their lives, making decisions, and watching their dreams come true. And me? I couldn't get out of bed, off the couch, or out of my closet. I'd try to hype myself up on the success of others, Pinterest quotes, and God's promises.

It worked sometimes. But then I'd be right back where I started. Back to overanalyzing, not only my situation but *why* I procrastinated, *why* I couldn't make decisions, or *why* I couldn't take consistent action. I'd loop around, like an American trying to maneuver a roundabout in Europe, shaming myself (believing it was motivation) into action. Eventually I'd work my way to an exit lane. I'd rally and knock out a good day's work, a tenacious workout, a week's worth of laundry, everything I'd put off (which compounds spectacularly in a home of six), only to be utterly exhausted the next day. Which, in turn, meant back to the couch. Repeat.

I didn't need hype. I needed clarity.

Avoidance Is Self-Sabotage

As I kept paying attention, the clues began to point to a pattern. A toxic cycle. I had been dissociating from my life—and there had to be a reason.

Eventually I could no longer rely on my introspection and reflection; I needed the Holy Spirit's revelation. I could see what I needed to change, but I needed Him to reveal the source, the root of my wounds, and I needed Him to keep showing me the Way.

Look at how John described the Holy Spirit:

> "But the Helper (Comforter, Advocate, Intercessor—Counselor, Strengthener, Standby), the Holy Spirit, whom the Father will send in My name [in My place, to represent Me and act on My behalf], He will teach you all things. And He will help you remember everything that I have told you."
>
> —John 14:26 AMP

He is the One who unlocks the door and turns on the lights in the forgotten spaces of our soul. *Over here,* He whispers. First walking through the door, then staying to sort things out—participating with us.

With the help of the Holy Spirit to peel back layer upon layer, clarification came. Underneath my fatigue, beyond the low energy levels, I discovered a false belief. Over time I had begun to believe life was all or nothing—there was no mode or speed in between. Fail or succeed. Fast or slow. Pain or promise. Amateur or expert. Broken or healed. Dreamer or doer. I had pitched my tent under the idea that if I put off the good things—what I wanted to work for—there was no room for failure or disappointment. I was learning the hard way that avoidance and procrastination are not self-protection or preservation; they are self-sabotage.

> Avoidance and procrastination are not self-protection or preservation, they are self-sabotage.

We must take an honest look and ask, *Do I withdraw from my life or do I live it?* I was withdrawing. I wasn't living; I was fighting my life. I was battling the things I couldn't control and avoiding the things I could control. Both led to self-sabotage.

My focus was on the lives of other people in my family, as well as strangers on the Internet that I was comparing myself to. I had been asleep to my own life, and the Holy Spirit was waking me up and inviting me to participate in *my* life.

Ways to Participate in Your Life

My eyes recently opened a wee bit wider upon reading what John O'Donohue has to say about awakening: "The self does not awaken

85

to find its purpose trapped in an isolated subjectivity, rather it awakens to ultimate participation."[2]

Coming alive is to participate. To participate is to come alive. *How, then, can we participate in our lives?*

Choosing to participate, for me, has looked like this:

- Reading a book on women and finances (it took two tries, but I did it)
- Staying in the room when I want to retreat (not easy when I feel offended)
- When I'm seeing all that is wrong, stopping to list (or speak) three things I'm grateful for
- Taking a shower (sometimes this simple action can make my day)
- Having a difficult conversation that I'd rather put off
- Completing a task that I've been avoiding (it could be as simple as scheduling an appointment)
- Making a decision and owning it (not second-guessing or being double-minded)

Avoidance is a choice. Procrastination takes work. Making no decision is a decision. The choice is ours. And today we can choose participation, practice, and peace.

I still may not be great with numbers, but facing them has inspired a few formulas of my own. Never mind that they are made of words.

Practice > Avoidance

Participation > Avoidance

CREATE SPACE

Meditate

*By Him you were called into companionship **and participation** with His Son, Jesus Christ our Lord.*

—1 CORINTHIANS 1:9 AMPC (EMPHASIS MINE)

Reflect

1. What has been overwhelming or exhausting you?
2. What have you been avoiding? Why?
3. What holds you back from taking action and participating in your life? Invite the Holy Spirit to reveal what you haven't been able to see—the root, the source of your pain. Write down what He shows you.

Act

Create your own participation list, then begin to work the list and participate in *your* life, starting today.

10

IMAGINE SPACE

*In very truth, a wise imagination, which is the
presence of the spirit of God, is the best guide that
man or woman can have; for it is not the things
we see the most clearly that influence us the most
powerfully.*

—George MacDonald[1]

You can have as much space as you need. Isn't that something
we all dream of, in one way or another?

More space.

More space to spread out. More room for our souls to breathe.

When our lives are cluttered, whether inside or out, it's hard to
see beyond the stuff. It's hard to imagine. Yet before the excess of
stuff there was space, space with endless potential.

I think of the times I've been house hunting. It's always strange and fascinating to tour other people's homes, to walk through the intimate space of another filled with their collections of life. Sometimes the homes are decorated beautifully, and the owner's belongings are lovely and proportionate to the house. Sometimes. Most times you have to look beyond the decor, furniture, paint colors, and clutter. You have to have eyes to see beyond what has been done and imagine what could be. With the removal of a wall, two small rooms might become a great room. With an addition built, a ranch could become a two-story home. Space can be imagined in different ways.

How do you imagine space?

By now I'm sure it's no surprise that I imagine space in the shape of homes. Old and stately, standing tall and wide for generations. Cottages, cozy and inviting, windows lit on a snowy winter's night. A ranch, lanky and long, separate wings adjoined. Curated living rooms. Empty rooms. Hidden halls. Conservatories. Studies lined with book-filled shelves. Tucked away closets. Secret spaces. The ability to add a wing, build up a second story, redesign, or remodel. With a home it isn't necessarily a matter of square footage, for a small home can be spacious and a grand home can be crowded. This is true of our lived-in and living homes as well. Homes, I've learned, are the framework that influence how we perceive, long for, and feel about space.[2]

Following World War II, C. S. Lewis, one of the brightest minds the world has seen, created space with his imagination—a land that millions upon millions have visited by way of their own imaginations: a place called Narnia. Lewis, too, imagined himself a living home. He said, "Imagine yourself as a living house. God comes in to rebuild that house."[3]

One might argue that Lewis's imagination was a gift that not everyone receives. He was brilliant and anointed for the work given to him—as are you. Lewis had a holy imagination—as do you. Lewis, however, was in the habit and practice of using his imagination. Won't you?

How content we become with what we are accustomed to. How skewed our vision for familiarity. How small our dreams due to inherited or learned mentalities, due to clutter we think we can't get rid of.

Lewis's words echo what God spoke in Isaiah 54:2: "Enlarge your house; build an addition. Spread out your home, and spare no expense!" (NLT). Imagine with me a wide-open space in your soul—more room in your life for the things that should be receiving your time and attention.

Observe You

Is your living home crowded? Cozy? Comfortable? Rigid? Expanding? Ready for a remodel? Condemned?

How we feel within our interior life directly correlates to how we view and respond to the exterior world. When I feel tight and cluttered on the inside, I tend to have eyes only for what's wrong externally—the messy house, the incomplete projects, the complications in relationships, the overwhelming workload.

I know it's hard to see clearly when we *feel* cluttered and overwhelmed. Sometimes we are met with situational tightness like a sudden bout with claustrophobia: a life-changing event; the surprise confrontation; the holiday gathering; an unexpected turn of events; a phone call that knocks the wind out of us. I've known this type of tightness to also be low-grade and lingering: chronic stress; unresolved tension in a relationship; impending change; financial strain; physical anxiety.

My soul has felt the constriction of clutter too. The weight—

both of my making and the acts of others toward me. Emotions so full they crowd out logic. Pain so visceral—sharp and dull, pounding and pinching—that it tingles to the ends of my fingers and toes. Memories stored so deep in the file cabinet of my sub-conscious that they overflow into my sleep. Particular people. Particular places. Anything unresolved within me. File drawers of unrealized dreams and ones I dare not vocalize. Folders filled with longings I can and cannot name. And records of happy times too. Inscriptions of joy. Color-coded good days. These dreams, stories, worries, hurts, memories, and longings run up and down the hallways of my heart and congregate in the rooms of my soul.

Are you willing to imagine? To practice seeing space? To let your mind wander beyond what is familiar?

Will you give yourself permission to hope and to dream?

For the longest time, I could not see.

Imagine my life better? My everyday better? I could not see how. I could not see a way. Out of that house. Out of dysfunction. Out of my own head. Out of pain. Out of situations and cycles that I had no control over. Out of patterns I didn't yet recognize, or couldn't admit existed. And out of patterns that might not have originated with me, yet I perpetuated them.

I could not see.

But God saw.

And other people saw. They saw and then they spoke.

I didn't believe them. I wouldn't allow myself. Because when we are desperate for hope, we view it as dangerous. The only thing scarier than having no hope is finding the courage to hope only to be met with disappointment. My soul might not have been able to accept truth, but my spirit was awakened and energized by truth. More space was available to me.

But before I could create space, I had to observe it.

Observe the Way

Our God is a God of expansion and growth. He is for the broad places and wide-open spaces. Therefore we must no longer allow ourselves to be deceived by a false sense of security or contentment, tucked up in our tight places. God is beckoning us to come out of hiding and to walk into an expansive life. He longs to expand your heart, your thinking, your vision, and your future. Will you give Him permission to work in you? To clear out and build out?

The Way is Jesus. He is the Way to a new and spacious life. It matters not what may be *in your way*, for *He is the Way*. Don't look back. Look to Jesus. He is doing something brand-new, and He wants you to see.

> *"Forget about what's happened;*
> *don't keep going over old history.*
> Be alert, be present. *I'm about to do something*
> *brand-new.*
> *It's bursting out! Don't you see it?*
> *There it is!* I'm making *a road through* the desert,
> rivers in the badlands."
> —Isaiah 43:19 (emphasis mine)

In our own effort to create space, it's our human nature to look back to the days before the clutter. Perhaps you recall things like

"Before trauma, I wasn't on high alert."
"Before I was so fearful, I lived my life without second-guessing my every move."
"Before depression, I was lighthearted and laughed all the time."
"Before the divorce, I wasn't afraid of rejection or being alone."

"Before the illness, I had energy."
"Before I lost my savings, I was secure."
"Before they died, I was joyful."

My thinking went like this:

"If I could just think more clearly—as I used to."
"If only I was as carefree as I was before life unraveled."
*"When things become normal again, then life won't feel so
heavy, so tight."*

Mistakenly, I believed that the key was returning to a simpler time or a different version of myself. I perceived myself experiencing spaciousness by remembering a time in which I felt I had more room.

At first my imagining was more like remembering. But there is a difference. Imagination is future forward, remembering is not. There is a time for remembering (Psalm 105:5). A time for going back in order to go forward—a necessary time for working through past wounds, old stories, decades of clutter. But before we do that, it is crucial to awaken your holy imagination and for your spirit—which completely understands newness and regeneration—to quicken to the truth that God wants to do a *new* thing and longs to take you to a *new* place.

God does not want new wine in the old wineskins.[4] He makes all things new.

New Covenant
New Earth
New Day
New Man
New Beginning

There is no space in yesterday for who you are today. It's time to reclaim our imagination for the good, for the new. To stop imagining all that could go wrong and imagine what could go right. To imagine what could be, more often than you remember what was.

Observe the Truth

God's love breaks open the way into a beautiful, broad place (Psalm 18:16–19). This means it's His work before it's ours. "Now to him who is able to do immeasurably more than all we ask or *imagine*, according to *his power that is at work within us*" (Ephesians 3:20 NIV, emphasis mine).

The *pressure* is not on you, *permission* is. Today, would you give God permission to work in you? Will you submit to His process—His way? Our prayer must be the same as that of the psalmist: God, I "give [you] the right to direct [my] life" (Psalm 37:5 TPT). I've prayed a version of that prayer my entire life, yet when the action of humble surrender finally met my words, my life became the prayer.

Praying those words in a posture of humble surrender cost me something. Surrender is hard to come by. It can take years to get there, but when we arrive, in an instant we are met with relief—relief and acceptance. From this place I remember feeling a pressure lift and space open up within me. It was no longer on me to figure out my life—how to change, how to get from *A* to *B*—it was on God. It was God's work, not mine. Now it was no longer about my problems; it was about His promise. Giving God permission relieves the pressure of what we were not meant to carry and clears the way.

Whether you are feeling ready to pull up your bootstraps and get going or you are feeling even more paralyzed, now that you have eyes to see the clutter you worked so hard to avoid, the Spirit of the Lord is here. And where the Spirit of the Lord is, there is freedom (2 Corinthians 3:17). In our finite minds it makes sense to get rid of clutter to create space, but with God, space is already here. There is freedom amid what you are bound by. There is space among the clutter and tight places. God *is* space and He lives in you.

In the thick of my tightness, when the eyes of my heart were clouded, my good Father kept asking me to open my eyes and observe. To see Him—space, light, zest—amid my personal soul clutter (Psalm 27:1). He helped me to see with these words, and I hope they will help you see too.

> [Insert your name here], *I am here.*
>   *Amid change, I am the same.*
>   *Amid unsettledness, I am settled in My love for you.*
>   *Amid trying to get it all done, I've done it all.*
>   *Amid your insecurity, I am secure.*
>   *Amid sickness, I am healing.*
>   *Amid weakness, I am strength.*
>   *Amid lack, I am abundance.*
>   *Amid endings, I am the beginning.*
>   *Amid darkness, I am light.*
>   *Amid grief, I collect your every tear.*
>   *Amid failure, I have given you unlimited fresh starts.*
>   *Amid death, I am new life.*
>   *Amid your rubble and ruins, I am restoring and redeeming.*
>   *Amid feeling out of control, I hold all things together.*
>   *Amid lies spoken about you, I not only know the truth—I am the Truth.*
>   *Amid worry, fear, and anxiety, I reign in your every situation (and potential scenario) as the Prince of Peace.*

The space I'm creating is beginning to emulate what I fought to see. Peace after a complicated conversation. Emotions that don't have the run of the house. Being open to change and new ideas. Room for joy on the difficult days. Capacity to care for my body. Time for family.

Can you imagine?

In this next section we will begin to own our lives—past, present, and future. Taking ownership of our pain, patterns, coping mechanisms, behavior, reactions—our clutter—is the pathway to overcoming a way of life that simply hasn't been working. Let's keep going!

CREATE SPACE

Meditate

He reached from on high, He took me;
He drew me out of many waters.

He rescued me from my strong enemy,
And from those who hated me, for they were too
  strong for me.

They confronted me in the day of my disaster,
But the LORD was my support.

He brought me out into a broad place;
He rescued me because He was pleased with me and
  delighted in me.
  —Psalm 18:16–19 AMP

Reflect

1. Where do you feel tight? What exactly does it feel like to you?
2. Dust off your imagination and imagine space in your soul. What does it look like? How do you feel?
3. Do you have a propensity to look back or look ahead? Why do you think that is? Ask God what "new thing" He wants you to see. Trust Jesus to be the Way.

Act

Imagine space by meditating on the truth of the scriptures in this chapter. Read them out loud. Read them slowly. Close your eyes. Imagine yourself doing what the Word says. Imagine the way through. Imagine God as space, enlarging your inner home amid the clutter.

Part two
Own

Owning our story and loving ourselves throughout that process is the bravest thing that we will ever do.

—Brené Brown[1]

11

TELL YOURSELF THE TRUTH

Above all, be the heroine of your life, not the victim.
—Nora Ephron[1]

Own. It's a petite word that holds a lot of power. I never realized how connected and disconnected I was to this word until I no longer owned a home.

Own is a word we all are familiar with. We own houses, stocks, cars, property, and businesses (although, let's be honest, most of us co-own everything with the bank). Essentially we work to own.

Growing up, I associated *own* with *business*. It was what my father did and still does. He owns newspapers. "What does your dad do?" always felt like a complicated question to answer when I was young. From my observation, he read newspapers and talked on the phone all day.

In my young and uneducated worldview, working was owning and owning was working. The two were enmeshed.

I understood early on the responsibility and time commitment owning a business entailed. There were rules and expectations that came with owning your own business. Of course, I didn't completely comprehend because I was ten; however, I had the aptitude to perceive the time and energy it took to be the owner. I perceived it because it affected me. I observed that as an owner, you woke up with the business on your mind. Certainly, your day was all about work, and the evenings were no exception—save dinner and a TV break. You then went to bed with the business on your mind—your reading material like a tiny mountain peak atop the nightstand. I was so proud of my dad and what he built—I still am. He worked, he studied, he took risks, he devised strategies and built something quite extraordinary.

To my surprise, my husband became a business owner too. I say *surprise* because he started out as a pastor. I thought we were going in the exact opposite direction of what I had always known. When we began having children, however, he started a business to supplement our income. He's an entrepreneur who happens to also love teaching, discipleship, ministering to people, and serving in the local church. He's a natural-born risk taker (constantly keeping me on the edge of my seat) and visionary, and he's brilliant with strategies and management. He's the hardest worker I know, and I'm so proud of what he's built. I can only imagine what he might dream up and build next.

Owning is not for the faint of heart.

Naturally, I grew up with a belief that we should work to own. In my teens and twenties, I tried to fight this way of life; I looked for a different way (marrying a pastor). In my thirties, I questioned it and then came to accept it as familiar—Stephen being a business owner. In my forties, I'm learning an entirely different definition of owning, which came by *not* owning—of no longer owning a home.

When we moved, we went from my childhood home to a rental home—long-standing to interim. I've never been great with change or transitions, and this one felt very jarring. I wasn't leaving my childhood home to go on to a forever home or a cool fixer-upper that we were taking on as a project. Essentially, I was making someone else's house my temporary home. We really didn't know what was next except that, for a season, we would be renting. We were in a stay-put kind of transition.

The rental market in my hometown was a doozy. Every online search ended with me in tears. Furthermore, we didn't have a date; we didn't know when, exactly, we would be moving. Physically I was living in my home, but mentally I was already living in the unknown. I was learning, like I never had before, what it meant to "wait on the Lord." I tried to remember that there was a promise attached, "But they that wait upon the LORD shall renew their strength; they shall mount up with wings as eagles; they shall run, and not be weary; and they shall walk, and not faint" (Isaiah 40:31 KJV). I needed strength.

I reminded myself over and over that God had never left me; He always made a way. I practiced recalling how He had been faithful to me. My mom would chime in and remind me when I'd forget. "God is faithful and this time will be no different," she would say. As only God can do, the right home became available at exactly the right time. We could bring our pets, we had enough room for our big family, and the property owner was kindhearted. The house was even surrounded by trees—God's kindness was tangible.

I have missed owning a home, decorating with abandon, being rooted to a place. I missed it before I ever left the old house. However, years before a move ever transpired, at the start of my soul cluttering up, the Lord spoke to me: *Home is not a place; it is a person. And that person is Jesus.*

"Yes, Lord, *You* are my home," I whispered.

My mouth spoke in what I believed to be true sincerity. Thus, it was not easy to discover that this was not the reality of my heart.

Own Your Inner Home

As we were moving, packing up items that had been in that home for decades—items that felt like they belonged to the home more than they belonged to me or my family—God began to show me that this next season was to be about owning my inner home. I didn't need to be focused on sourcing new furniture, plotting DIYs, building gallery walls, or obsessing over the next house I hoped to own. Instead, I was to work with what was sitting upon the shelves of my soul. Were there walls that needed to be torn down? What memorabilia would I not let go of? Did I need a redesign or a remodel? Would I work with the bones of my home? Could I own any complicity for the clutter in my soul?

A little over a year later, my dear friend Mindi invited me to Seaside, Florida, for a girls' trip. I was the only introvert on the trip, so I gladly accepted the single room and was happy to wake up early to have thinking time on the covered porch of the darling Airbnb where we were staying. It was picture perfect, so much so that I remembered that Seaside is where they filmed *The Truman Show.*

My eyes took in the pastel-colored coastal homes while my soul drank in the beauty of the surrounding nature. Before I knew it, I was traveling into my well-worn daydream of a place of my own, wishing that one of these lovely houses were mine. Just as I was getting carried away, taking a sudden turn in my daydream travels toward frustration for my life not going according to plan, I was reminded of something Myquillyn Smith posted on Instagram. She said, "Admire it without needing to acquire it."[2] I let those words sink down into the file cabinets of my soul. *I don't need to own something to appreciate and enjoy it.* There I was back to that word again: *own.* Why did I want to own a home so badly? Owning made me feel safe. Owning made me feel like somebody (I don't mean this in a pretentious way, but a tangible one)—somebody who had a place where they belonged, a place they felt settled, a place where their roots could grow deep.

I returned to the place where I was, feeling the sticky breeze upon my skin, staring off into the pines that reminded me more of Georgia than Florida. I remembered that all I thought I owned was never mine to begin with; it's all God's, and it always has been (the earth is the Lord's and everything in it—Psalm 24:1).

Own yourself, I heard Him whisper. *Your actions. Your attitudes. Your behavior. Your choices. There is no decorating right now—other than your heart and soul.*

I own my choices and their outcomes. I own my actions. I own my attitudes. I own my behavior. I own the opportunity to do something about all my pain, all my clutter—this is my responsibility.

Accepting Truth Takes Courage

If we want lasting change, it's time to own up—to take ownership.

What does it even mean to own yourself, to own up?

The *Cambridge Dictionary* defines *owning up* as "to tell the truth or to admit that you are responsible for something."[3] Do you remember having to own up when you got in trouble as a kid? I do. To overcome, first we must own. We have to tell the truth and take responsibility. We aren't responsible for what was done to us. However, we are responsible for what we choose to do with our pain. It can seem like the opposite—as if your pain owns you. Nevertheless, it can only own you if you give it that power. If you choose to take ownership for your spiritual, mental, and emotional health, you will begin to heal.

Will you choose healing or living with toxicity?

It's easy to blame.

It takes courage to own, because accepting truth takes courage.

Most people choose delusion because it is comfortable. They avoid truth because it's uncomfortable.

God's responsibility is to set free—which is already done by the completed work of the cross. While God has already completed the work of freedom and it is ours, we often find that there is a process and path to experiencing the fullness of freedom.

Our responsibility is to own.

However, as we are learning, God is always looking for our participation.

Look at these life-changing words in Isaiah 52:2 (NIV): "Free yourself from the chains on your neck, Daughter of Zion, now a captive." We know that our freedom is paid for. That the great wide-open awaits us. Yet if we don't remove the chains, if we don't walk out of the tight spaces, we aren't experiencing the abundant life Christ paid for. It's not the fairy wand that vanishes the chain; it's the child of God who understands their freedom enough to slide the broken chain off.

> If we don't remove the chains, if we don't walk out of the tight spaces, we aren't experiencing the abundant life Christ paid for.

Piece by piece, box by box, I'm owning up to what God reveals in the hidden places of my heart and soul, to what I already know and choose to avoid, to what my loved ones point out.

None of it is easy. It's humbling to tell your children "You are responsible for your response and reactions" only to realize that you, yourself, are not taking responsibility for talking unkindly, for spiraling out of control, for being selfish, for blaming others for your actions. I'm teaching this to my children because I want them to become functioning, interdependent adults. I want them to be able to remove the chains and unpack the boxes of their soul clutter too.

I believe this is why God walks us through the *process* of freedom. We are His children and He is our Father. I want my children to grow up to lead, to help others, and to advance God's kingdom in their unique callings. God wants these very things for us. Our participation and cooperation (obedience) is an indicator of our maturity and desire to grow. No matter our age or state, God will never stop parenting us; He will never give up on us. Furthermore, our unique callings and purposes do not expire.

What if our soul clutter originates from something that was done to us or that we happened to be in the wake of?

For instance, chronic stress may come from a situation that is completely out of your control. This was the case for me. Remember, it took my body freaking out for me to begin to connect the dots and own up that the two were connected. For a long while I couldn't even admit that. What was clear to others was foggy for me. I needed the torchlight of God's love to cut through the dense fog and reveal what was right in front of me. Then I had to begin to own up to how I might be contributing to the stress. Its origin may have been out of my control, but my response to it is within my control. Am I going to bed on time? Am I eating too much junk food (my go-to when I'm stressed)? Am I moving my body? Am I feeding the drama or starving it? Am I establishing and keeping to my boundaries?

> No matter our age or state, God will never stop parenting us; He will never give up on us.

To help you think about what you need to begin to own, I'm sharing a list of things I've had to own in my life, along with actions I'm taking; owning requires responsibility and commitment.

Recently I went through the process of owning my depression. Naming depression was not easy for me. It was one of those "If I don't say it, it's not real" things in my life. I own my depression by making a choice to lay this at the feet of Jesus. I believe for healing *and* I participate in that process. Participating has looked like counseling, studying, replenishing my depleted soul, not fighting myself when hormones are at the monthly peak, nurturing and nourishing my body, strategizing for joy, and owning every little trace of a victim mentality.

Please note that talking about a victim mentality is tender. Some of us have a victim mentality because we have been a victim of abuse. If we were to talk face-to-face, Dear Reader, you would feel my compassion, you'd see tears well up, and you'd hear the gentleness in my voice. If you have been a victim of abuse, there is nothing that you've done wrong. You are not responsible for what was done to you. I am so sorry that you have endured abuse. By the kindness of God, I've learned that it does not serve me well to continually identify as a victim. We are more than what has been said or done to us. I do not want this to be my identity. Nor do I want it to be the lens that I see everything through. Christ has called me a victor. Christ calls you a victor (1 John 5:4 AMP).

I hope you're beginning to see the progress that you're making. You've done the work to inventory your clutter, you're listening to your body, you're aware of your emotional age, you've agreed to get uncomfortable, and you're participating in enlarging your home. Now, as you begin to own the truth and own your cluttered soul, you'll be empowered to move forward in strength. Truth is the only way to freedom (John 8:32).

Things I've had to own	How I'm taking action
My contribution to stress (lack of sleep, proper nourishment, rest, drama)	Evaluate my choices with intellectual honesty and make adjustments
My propensity to emotionally spiral when life feels out of control	Recognize it, breathe, lead my thoughts and actions
My sharp tongue: lashing out or being critical	Practice holding my tongue and listening (Proverbs 10:19)
Nagging or complaining	Encourage others and offer ideas and solutions
Codependent behaviors and people pleasing	Practice accepting that not everyone will be happy with me or my choices
Shutting down or escaping when things become too hard	Engage by staying in the room, conversating, finishing the task at hand
Escalating disagreements	Practice defusing disagreements or returning to a conversation later
Self-pity	Practice gratitude by listing what is good and right in my life
Avoidance, excuses, and procrastination	Participate in small ways. Make decisions. Don't wait for things to align, just begin.
People being my source, rather than God	Thank God for supplying my needs
Negativity	Smile. Exercise to release endorphins
Depression	Nourish my body, soul, and spirit
Victim mentality	Notice and name the choices I can make
Unhealthy coping mechanisms	Identify and engage in a healthy coping mechanism

CREATE SPACE

Meditate

Blessed and greatly favored is the man whose
strength is in You,
In whose heart are the highways to Zion.

Passing through the Valley of Weeping (Baca), they
make it a place of springs;
The early rain also covers it with blessings.

They go from strength to strength [increasing in
victorious power];
Each of them appears before God in Zion.
—Psalm 84:5–7 AMP

Reflect

1. Are you more apt to blame or take responsibility? If your soul clutter did not originate with you, are you able to take responsibility for your response and removing the chains that Christ has broken?
2. Have you been finding comfort in delusions? What are they?
3. Are there any areas in which you are being complicit in your clutter (contributing to your stress, worry, anxiety, etc.)? How?

Act

After prayer and pondering, create your own list of what you need to begin owning. This doesn't mean you have to tackle everything at once. This means you have found the courage to tell yourself the truth.

12

EMBRACE MYSTERY

—————

The mystery of life isn't a problem to solve, but a reality to experience.

—Frank Herbert, *Dune*[1]

I am a bit of a mystery junkie. I love to read them; I love to watch them. It's important that you know I did not read one Nancy Drew book as a kid. I was more of the Sweet Valley Twins kind of girl. I also feel you should know that I don't like gruesome mysteries. I prefer "cosy crime." (And it's necessary that we use the *s* rather than a *z* because this genre is chiefly British and because I am a good Anglophile.) Cosy crime, according to the *Independent*, is a subgenre of crime spawned by the great Agatha Christie (who, according to her great-grandson, would not like murder being considered "cosy" in any way), in which "a dead body is a puzzle, an enigma, a knot just waiting for a clever sleuth to come along and unravel it and save the day."[2]

These mysteries are considered cosy because they often take place in a village, a small town, or within an intriguing manor home or estate. The characters are quirky, interesting, and some quite affable. You're always sure to find either an unlikable detective who somehow manages to be endearing, or a clever busybody type in the village who fancies themselves a sleuth.

I became a mystery fanatic when there was no answer to when my parents' divorce might finalize, when I didn't know how much longer my grandpa would live or when we'd move out of our house. When I didn't know if or when an illness I was experiencing would pass. When I didn't know if my loved one would even make it out of the hospital. When I didn't know if an important relationship in my life was repairable. When I couldn't see the end to what was nearly a decade of loss, change, uncertainty, depression, and anxiety.

Call it a coping mechanism if you will; it did help me. Working hard to solve someone else's mystery gave me a focus and a good distraction from fixating on what I had no control over. It helped to have closure and conclusions with the turn of a page.

What do we do with what doesn't make sense? With what was supposed to happen but didn't? With what was unexpected or unfair?

We often engage in a process that goes something like this. We begin with the two prayers that never seem to get answered: "Why?!" and "When?!" Then, tired from plodding through grief, anger, worry, or frustration, we reluctantly settle down to a big stack of books or Internet scrolling. We see therapists (which is good and necessary) and talk ourselves in circles with family and friends, dissecting details, looking for anything that was missed—just one small clue.

With persistence and a keen eye, chances are we will uncover something. A clue. A piece to the puzzle. A diagnosis. A story we never knew that somehow makes sense of our own. And it will help until we realize there is still so much mystery. We may even indulge in our own personal family detective work—getting to the bottom of *some* things—including a few things we wish we wouldn't have uncovered—and yet there is still so much that is inconclusive and will remain so this side of heaven. The question is, can we own the mystery?

Mystery begins at a young age. As a child do you remember venturing out of your world into a friend's home for a sleepover? A different family, a new home, a strange environment—mysterious origins. Suddenly, at a tender age, we begin to notice that life is different and people live differently. As we grow up, we gain curiosity of what our lives could look like. There is possibility. It's *all* a mystery (in a good way).

That's why we played games like MASH (the paper game that determined who you would marry, what kind of car you would drive, and what type of home you would live in—Mansion, Apartment, Shack, House): to give parameters to the unknowns and vast variations of adulthood. (I can tell you now that I don't live in either a shack or a mansion, and I did not marry Kirk Cameron.)

We grow further into teen years where we are convinced we have it all figured out. We formulate that possibility + potential = probability. We plan. We dream. We are convinced we are in control. At least I was convinced. "If I make *this* choice, then I will get *that* outcome." This is what I believed.

Teenage Trina was precious. She was idealistic, hopeful, and disciplined. But she was also a bit of a judgmental know-it-all (the only thing she didn't know was that she wasn't smarter than her parents). Then we become adults and realize that not all potential and planning equates to the outcomes we dreamed of and strived for. Reality sets in. Sometimes slow and steady and other times abrupt and jarring. Our questions outnumber our certainties, and our worries become more detailed than our carefully curated ten-year plans.

- What if I'm laid off?
- What if I don't get married?
- Will the world ever return to a semblance of normal?
- Will I ever be able to recover financially?
- Will this relationship ever be restored?
- Will this depression ever end?
- Will I recover from this illness?
- Will they ever quit drinking?
- Will everything really be okay?
- If I just knew!

Because if I just knew how it turns out, I'd know how to deal. If I just knew he was going to change in a year (or never change, for that matter), I'd know how to proceed. If I just knew how the judge would rule, I could prepare. If I just knew my job was secure, I'd have peace of mind.

I spent a good part of the past ten years in a dark mystery (that is a long time!) asking similar questions to the ones listed above. It was the not-knowing that overwhelmed me. I believed it would be easier to buckle down and handle things dragging on for another five years than to not know and have it last only one more year.

Not knowing is not only overwhelming, it is exhausting. Working hard to understand takes a lot of energy. When you are living in some form of in-between, you are shrouded in a dense and drippy fog. No matter how hard you try to make sense of what doesn't make sense, things are never quite as they seem. In the fog you bump up to what feels like closure or conclusion only to find that the trail doesn't stop there; the twists and turns continue on and on.

I'm still living within a few open-ended questions and story lines from the aforementioned decade, but I have come to a few conclusions and learned approaches to make peace with the unknown.

Make Peace with What Doesn't Make Sense

Our lives are a mystery; the sooner we make peace with that, the sooner we progress.

Dear Reader, we don't have to have all the answers to live fully, today.

Here is the hope: The author of our stories is God (our Good Father, the Creator, the Master Artist, Author, and Finisher). He is the original author and master storyteller. And with Him, the ending is good. If we read the Bible, then we know how the story ends: the bad guys are caught and justice is served.

> Our lives are a mystery; the sooner we make peace with that, the sooner we progress.

A few years ago, in my dark fog, God reminded me that I am not the author—He is. After He spoke those words to my spirit, I twirled in my office chair in an assured stupor, thinking, *Whoa! Well, I may be a legit author writing* about *my life, but I'm not the author* of my life. I had to write it out on a sticky note (I'm all about the sticky notes) to remind myself in the midst of great uncertainty and insecurity.

I am not the author of my story—God is.

Do you need this reminder too?

Disclaimer: This does not mean that we don't plan, make good choices, and work to create a good and purposeful life. Strategy, wisdom, prayer, and action (hard work) yield good fruit. We are made in the image of the Creator, and He invites us to co-create with Him. We have the power to create change. We don't, however, have the power to control (other people or outcomes).

Look for the Clues

That's right, I said it. Go ahead and look for clues. Only, the clues that I recommend looking for are the clues God designed for you. You'll recognize them because they are much more to do with you and your growth than with the outcome of others.

As you might have already surmised, I rather like to consider myself a sleuth (with all the hours I've logged with my British murder mysteries). Perhaps I should consider calling myself a sleuth of the soul. I think we all should be the sleuth of our own soul. It simply requires seeing what others seem to miss. It means you delight in the details and you ask the right questions. (They usually begin with *what* rather than *why*.)

Here are a few questions to get you started:

1. What would You have me learn from this inconclusive situation?
2. What could I have done differently?
3. What are You speaking to *me*?
4. What is the fruit? Is there *evidence* of God's work in me (Galatians 5)?
5. What details do I need to see? The mysteries we need to give our attention to are the secrets hidden in God's ways.
6. What is my next step?

Own Your Need to Understand

While I'll always seek and desire to understand things, I've realized there are things I may never fully understand. And above seeking understanding, I seek to trust God. Proverbs 3:5 is clear that we are to trust in God with all our heart and lean not on our own understanding. We have to take ownership of our need to understand and our desire to control

> Above seeking understanding, I seek to trust God.

our circumstances. When we lay down those burdens (because they are burdens), we can live lighter and freely. The psalmist beautifully described that when we abandon ourselves to God, we enter into the mystery (Psalm 40:1–3).

I still prefer mysteries to be in books and on TV, but with each day I'm learning to live peacefully within the mystery and to own my not knowing. Like a seasoned investigator, I love looking for clues that God leaves me everywhere.

These days, if I'm itchy to solve a mystery, I watch *Father Brown*.

CREATE SPACE

Meditate

We don't yet see things clearly. We're squinting in a fog, peering through a mist. But it won't be long before the weather clears and the sun shines bright! We'll see it all then, see it all as clearly as God sees us, knowing him directly just as he knows us!

—1 CORINTHIANS 13:12

Reflect

1. Are you living your life or just trying to solve it?
2. What open-ended question(s) or mystery has your soul clutter presented you with?
3. Have you been leaning on your own understanding? Do you need to trust God more?

Act

There is nothing foggy about the fact that life will be filled with mystery. In fact, God is quite clear about it. Our understanding in the here and now is simply incomplete. What is clear is that God understands everything about *you*. Ask Him for clues! Thoughtfully answer the questions listed under "Look for the Clues" above. This week begin to be a sleuth of your soul by looking for the clues God has hidden just for *you*, and then take the next right step.

13

BE A THOUGHT LEADER

*You are today where your thoughts have brought
you; you will be tomorrow where your thoughts take
you.*

—James Allen[1]

"Just tell me what you are afraid of." My dad kept asking, late into the winter night. I didn't want to answer; I didn't want to say it. But I knew I had to give him something.

"A dragon!" I blurted. "A dragon," I lied. It seemed like a normal thing an eight-year-old should be afraid of. I couldn't say what I was really afraid of because I didn't want to form the words and say them. Somewhere in my child's mind I knew that any adult would rationalize my fear away. "Oh yes, that is horrible," they would say. "But you don't have to be afraid of that. It's not going to happen to you. It doesn't have anything to do with you. You are safe." They would find the irrational fear of a nonexistent beast more rational than what was making me wander in circles and unable to climb under my covers. I was afraid of the *Challenger* explosion.

It was 1986, and the space shuttle *Challenger* had just exploded over Cape Canaveral, Florida. I first learned of this tragedy at school. I couldn't tell you if we watched it live on TV in our classroom, as many kids my age remember, because if we did, I've blocked it out. Perhaps my teacher only announced it to us? It's likely since that is the part I will never forget. Mrs. Sanders's description of the tragedy was horrifying. I can still see her. Her eyes squinting through the iconic '80s oversized, round plastic-rimmed glasses that she wore every day. Her hair short, dark, and wavy. Her fingers wiggling as she said, "There are fingers and toes floating everywhere in the ocean." Her voice moody and frightening, as if reading us a Grimms fairy tale.

Maybe it was weird to be afraid of fingers and toes floating in the ocean when I lived smack dab in the middle of the country, in the middle of cornfields. But I imagined those broken bodies, those fingers and toes everywhere—under my covers, under my bed, on the floor, behind the door. You see why it was just easier to fear the dragon.

As fate would have it, my family had a trip planned to Florida a few months later. We went to Disney. We went to the beach. While my siblings were happy to play in the sand and splash in the water, my little eight-year-old self was busy trying to figure out where I had heard of "Cocoa Beach" before. That night at the hotel, the dots connected, like they did on my Lite-Brite. The *Challenger*. I would not go to bed. I would not get under the covers. I could not sit still. I literally jumped from bed to bed like I was playing a game of "the floor is lava" (only I didn't even know about that game in the '80s). My poor parents. They had far more patience than I would as a parent. My mom finally calmed me down, and it was in that hotel room that I had to tell them about the fingers and toes and what Mrs. Sanders had said.

What was happening back then (although I didn't understand it at the time) is what I still have an inclination to do: let my mind spiral. When I spiral I tend to take a thought, often irrational, and keep it to myself until I'm to the point of almost hysterics (sometimes over the hypothetical) and, clearly, I can hide no more. My mom pointed out this pattern and coined the term "shuttle thinking." These days I don't jump from bed to bed, but I tend to jump from thought to thought. From worry to worry. From fear to fear. And, in times of great stress and soul clutter, from panic to panic.

Stop the Spiral

In recent years, living through a global pandemic, we have collectively experienced fear and scarcity. We've all met immutable thoughts and anxieties, ones in which we've shared a commonality. There has been scarcity of certainty, of community, of security, of health. If we all shared our unique stories, I believe we would discover more similarities than differences. Each and every one of us the world over has been worried about their health and the health of the ones they love.

I recall a night when I awoke with a very upset stomach and a headache. Normally it wouldn't have been reason for alarm or for my thoughts to run amok except that in this day and age a twinge is no longer a twinge. A runny nose is nary a cold. We've learned to be vigilant in observing symptoms of any sort. And, as it turns out, it's no easy feat to separate being on alert from being anxious. I was on alert because I had been around loved ones who were ill.

Besides these newfangled worries, my thoughts always seem to circle back to that horrible reaction I had to that antibiotic. I never gave a thought to my liver prior to that event, but now that organ of mine asserts itself to the fore of my mind. With the churn of my stomach, my thoughts began to gang up on me and I started getting shaky (my indication of a panic attack). I sat on the bathroom floor, too scared to take medicine because what if that caused more problems, and worked on breathing deep. I prayed. I walked myself through logical reasoning. I practiced redirecting my thoughts.

However, the middle of the night is always a precarious time when it comes to the mind. Nothing is as it seems in the dark. Truth is hidden. Lies magnify. Over the years I've learned that it's best to voice the fears, no matter how ridiculous they sound, because when we voice them, we can then voice truth over them. I ended up in the bathroom at 2:00 a.m. calling my mom (since moms are used to being woken up in the middle of the night). I went through it all. Thought to thought. Worry to worry. Like, bed to bed. When I got to "What if my liver . . ." she stopped me and said, "Trina! You're spiraling! Stop the shuttle thinking." "Mom," I said, "weird, I was going to write about that in the morning."

We went through pretty much the same process I went through on my own, only we did it together. Then we talked about nothing for almost an hour because my mom is the greatest. She prayed for me, reminded me to resist the Enemy—immediately—and then recommended I download the Abide app that my sister uses in the wee hours of the morning when her narcolepsy won't let her sleep (yes, I got that right—it's hard to stay awake during the

> It's best to voice the fears, no matter how ridiculous they sound, because when we voice them, we can then voice truth over them.

day and hard to sleep at night). It took a while, but with the meditative sleep story "I Am Secure" playing, I was able to slowly go back to sleep.

Lead Your Thoughts

One way I sort through my mental clutter is to redirect. Redirect like you would a person headed the wrong way. Redirect like you would a child fixated on something trivial. Redirect your route like you would when you know a storm could be avoided.

The Bible shows us that we *can* lead every thought captive into the obedience of Jesus Christ (2 Corinthians 10:5). It also tells us that we can fix our thoughts on what is beautiful, including every glorious work of God (Philippians 4:8). This means our thoughts shouldn't lead us; we should lead them.

Where are your thoughts leading you?

If you have a habit of your thoughts running wild and you find yourself following them blindly—around the corner, down dark hallways, and through dark basements—don't be discouraged! I want you to know today that you have the capability to lead and to own those thoughts with the help of the Holy Spirit.

One way I redirect my thoughts is by flipping the script. If I catch myself focusing on what is missing and what is wrong, I do a full stop and look for what is right and good. Sometimes I have to do this within the first few minutes of waking. I have to begin uncluttering right away before the negative thoughts set the tone for my day, making me feel boxed in and unable to move.

I spent years feeling ashamed that my mind goes negative the minute I wake up. In flipping the script, I've had to take my eyes off perfection and turn them toward the glory of progress. And I'm making progress by observing these patterns in my life and then taking ownership of how I respond to negative thoughts, worry, overwhelm, and the like. I'm overcoming by giving my attention to what is right and cleaning up my mental clutter.

Getting out of your head is one of the best ways to lead and redirect your thoughts. To get out of your head, simply move your body. Movement of any kind does wonders in clearing out mental clutter. An overworked mind often results in a standstill of both the mind and body. To break this cycle, try a walk. Fresh air is preferable, and nature also gives us the easy opportunity to fix our thoughts on the beautiful. If you can't make it outside, I find a treadmill works too. Physicist and Nobel Prize winner Eugene Wigner was often seen wandering through the campus of Princeton. In the book *Rest*, he is quoted as saying, "My mind often comes to a standstill after some hours indoors. So I take a walk. Outside, my mind immediately begins to move freely and instinctively over my subject. Ideas come rushing to my mind, without being called. Soon enough, the best answer emerges from the jumble. I realize what I can do, what I should do, and what I must abandon."[2]

In the dark of night, when a walk is not an option and nothing seems to be working, call in for reinforcements. Thoughts that are shaped in worry and framed in fear are not merely wispy wanderings or ephemeral matter; they are tendril-esque, weedy things, trying to take root and spread into the good soil of your soul. These thoughts, which often form into patterns, beliefs, and neural pathways, grow in the dark.

Don't keep your soul clutter in the dark; shine the light by reaching out for help from a spouse, a counselor, a parent, a trusted friend, and always from the Holy Spirit—our ever-present help. Someone helping you lead your thoughts captive is not a sign of failure or weakness—it's the promise of a good return: "Two are better than one, because they have a good return for their labor: If either of them falls down, one can help the other up" (Ecclesiastes 4:9–10 NIV).

Thought to captivity.
Worry to peace.
Overwhelm to clarity.
Your thoughts don't own you; you own them.

CREATE SPACE

Meditate

And we lead every thought and purpose away captive into the obedience of Christ (the Messiah, the Anointed One).

—2 CORINTHIANS 10:5 AMPC

Reflect

1. Are you leading your thoughts or are your thoughts leading you?
2. Where are your thoughts leading you? What is causing you to spiral?
3. Who in your life can help you lead your thoughts when you need support?

Act

We can't always help when a thought pops up, but we can own our response to it. We can recognize when we are spiraling and ask for help.

1. Reach out to someone if your thoughts are overwhelming you.
2. Be intentional to notice and make note of what is good and right in your life.
3. Try taking a walk to clear out mental clutter.

14

DECLARE YOUR DECISIONS

~~~~~~~~~

Most people don't lead their life, they accept their life.
—John C. Maxwell[1]

When I was a kid, my creativity was best embodied by all the pretend businesses I started. Some of them weren't actually pretend. Like the time I started "Dial-A-Number" with my best neighborhood pals Judy and Laurie. The concept was that if you needed a phone number, you called us (on my home landline) instead of calling 411 (known as directory assistance for information in the pre-Internet days). We'd then look up the phone number (in the phone book) and give it to you. Then you'd leave ten cents in my mailbox. Brilliant, right? The only call we ever got was from Judy and Laurie's dad, who wanted the phone number of President Bush. Stumped. But he still left a dime in the mailbox.

Whether a pretend business or some unsuccessful money-making attempt of mine, I was always the kid with an entrepreneurial idea and I always had to be the boss. I unashamedly attempted to be the boss of everything and everyone (let's blame this on my birth order).

Some days I am the one who is most surprised that I didn't grow up to be a business boss. I think Judy and Laurie might both be surprised at how my personality has shifted through the years. (I wonder if they would still see traces of ten-year-old me.) Somewhere along the way I realized that being a boss wasn't working for me.

With age, I learned to shift from bossing to leading, and I did well with that for some time. In high school I was a cheer*leader*. In my youth group, which saw more than one thousand students and young adults in attendance each week, I was a student leader. I helped launch our school newspaper, and I was, apparently, a vote away from homecoming queen (don't ask how I know). In college I led a high school small group and was in the core leadership of my youth group.

Once newly married, Stephen and I started and led a church, and not long after, I began working for leadership guru John Maxwell. In that season I began to believe that perhaps I was not cut out to lead. It was a gradual shift. Quiet little sometimes-subconscious agreements that I made with myself.

Clearly I wasn't cut out to lead people in our church because they were older, and back then leading as a pastor's wife meant singing and playing the piano. That certainly was not my skill set. Instead, I made myself small and hid behind the overhead projector. At work I noticed very quickly how sharp my coworkers were. They were only a few years older than me and leading entire departments and eventually the company. Outside of my bubble of origin, I found it was easier to go along, to get along. I began to back down on wanting to lead because I noticed that there were others who liked to lead more than I did and were more inclined to do so. They were naturally assertive and outspoken.

Life went along, seemingly fine, until I realized that I was letting life happen to me and allowing circumstances and others to dictate my decisions. I was being agreeable because I wanted to be likable. It's not that I didn't have opinions or couldn't make decisions; it's that I wanted everyone to be happy, and I didn't want anyone to be upset with me—classic people pleasing. I have strong values and I'm extremely steadfast, to the point of being called stubborn by those whom I wouldn't budge for. I prefer to think more than I talk, and I'm not going to battle someone who really wants to be (or seems to have a need to be) in charge.

Now I understand and own that it has been my choice to go along, to people please, to not speak up, to presume that others were better at leading, to believe that I wasn't smart enough or strong enough or connected enough. This was a form of avoidance.

One day I woke up—smack in the middle of my emotional maturing, my owning up, my growing up—and realized, "Hey, I'm the boss of *me*." My focus had been on who was the boss of who, when it should have been on me being the boss of me. I had a better revelation of this when I was elementary age than I did at forty years old. I decided it was time to awaken my inner ten-year-old. Here I am at forty-three, the boss of my life, chief of ideas and execution. I own everything that has happened to me—the good, the bad, the ugly—by way of my own actions and by way of others' actions toward me. I own my choices, my behavior, my decisions, and the outcomes. I am no longer just a responsible person; I'm a person who takes responsibility for my life.

I thought I wasn't the boss type anymore because I believed

- I'm not assertive.
- I don't like confrontation.
- I'm slow at (and sometimes afraid of) making decisions.
- Other people might not like me.
- I'm not a risk taker.
- I don't have what it takes.
- I'm too sensitive.

In my owning up, I'm learning that

- I can have hard conversations.
- Not all confrontation is negative.
- Every decision doesn't require me laboring over it ("Done is better than perfect"[2]).
- It's okay if everyone doesn't like me (that's not the goal).
- I can practice taking risks.
- Being sensitive gives me different advantages.

I don't really think it's my dream to be a business boss anymore, yet I have no idea what the future holds. I do know, with certainty, that if I can't be the boss of me, I will never be a good boss to other people. If I can't take action in my own life, I won't be able to lead others in action. If I can't make decisions personally, I'll struggle to make them professionally. If I can't lead myself, I have no business leading others. To unclutter our souls, we have to take our eyes off others. We must release the clutter of comparing ourselves with others, competing with others, and trying to control others. The new #goal is to be the boss of our own lives. Here's how we can begin.

How to Be the Boss of Your Life

1. **Practice > Avoidance (Remember our formula?)** I've concluded that avoidance stems from perfectionism. Trying to get things as close as possible to perfect sounds noble, yet it's anything but. Avoidance will get you absolutely nowhere; imperfect practice will take you further than you think.

2. **Grow as you go.** No one knows off the bat how to be a boss—not even of themselves. When my dad bought his first newspaper, he was a junior in college. The majority of his employees were older, and he had to learn to manage them on the fly.

3. **Take a risk.** Don't like taking risks? Me neither. Last year, in an effort to be the boss of my life, I read a book about women and money called *Worth It*. I learned all kinds of things about investing, but what really stuck with me and will help shape my boss behavior are these four simple words: "Inaction is a risk."[3] You see, everything is a risk, including not taking them. What's causing you to pause?

4. **Make decisions.** Easier said than done, right? There have been times in life when I'd drag my feet and my dad would chime in, "No decision is a decision." I now have those words written on a sticky note (surprise!) that hangs just above the silly "Girl Boss" plaque on my desk. My sister bought the plaque to remind me that I really like being a boss (she's taken the brunt of my bossing her entire life—and still, she loves me). Leading your life is the accumulation of one small decision upon another to participate in your day.

5. **Know the difference between action and motion.** In the book *Atomic Habits*, author James Clear points out a distinction between motion and action: "When you're in motion, you're planning and strategizing and learning. Those are all good

things, but they don't produce a result. Action, on the other hand, is the type of behavior that will deliver an outcome." He goes on to say, "Motion is useful, but it will never produce an outcome by itself. . . . motion allows us to feel like we're making progress without running the risk of failure."[4] Uncluttering your soul is a continual process. It's not an event; it's a habit of action that anyone can develop.

6. **Don't be afraid to fail; you will.** Failure is only failure if you quit. Otherwise, failure is simply data. And data is information. And such personalized information about ourselves plays a role in our transformation. Decluttering is hard work. You'll get tired; learn to take a break instead of quitting. Decluttering is strategic; however, the strategy is best learned in the doing. As you find what doesn't work, you'll discover what does. Just keep at it.

Taking action and responsibility are never easy, but it turns out that being the boss of your own life is pretty great. Making decisions dispels clutter and creates clarity. Taking risks will empower you to take more. Wins build our confidence, and the losses teach us not only how to calculate and strategize better but that we can indeed survive failure and keep going.

CREATE SPACE

Meditate

"You're blessed when you get your inside world—your mind and heart—put right. Then you can see God in the outside world."
—MATTHEW 5:8

Reflect

1. What thoughts or beliefs have you had about yourself as a leader or boss?
2. Give yourself a review. What areas are you winning in? Which need improvement? Bosses are into metrics and reports. Profit-and-loss statements are a must. When it comes to the soul, fruit is our great metric. Would you report gains (a harvest of fruit according to Galatians 5) or a loss?
3. Who or what have you allowed to boss you? Social media? A well-meaning friend? Bad beliefs?

Act

Take action. Tackle one thing, big or small, that you have been avoiding. Make a decision. Take a risk. Practice what you've been putting off because you want it to be perfect. Not sure what you have been avoiding? What is that one thing that keeps rolling over day after day, week after week, on your to-do list? What is one thing you would do if you weren't afraid to fail?

15

DESIGN NEW PATTERNS

Clutter is the enemy of clarity.
—Julia Cameron[1]

Patterns. I much prefer this word in terms of design—the perfect combination of colors, textures, and eye-catching layers, cozying up the perfect home environment. For me, I picture an English country home, tucked in the trees down a long pea-gravel drive that crunches and crackles under the rubber of tires and rain boots all the same.

Upon entering the blue-painted door, one is met with an array of textures, textiles, colors, and patterns. Muted botanical wallpaper, a colorful English roll-arm sofa dressed in floral and splattered with ikat, polka-dot, and toile patterned pillows. Across from the sofa are softly striped and slipcovered twin chairs complete with ruffled skirts. A fabric ottoman draped with a suzani sits functionally between, to hold tea and time. A Turkish rug boasting rich color and hand-stitched patterns sits on a textured sisal rug that grounds everything atop it. Tables are topped with bold blue, Oriental-patterned ginger jars and brass lamps that glow in the night, illuminating delicate fairy-esque flowers on their crinkle-cut shades. Books are everywhere: in rows on the shelves, stacked on the tables, piled on the floor, tucked between a cushion. Should you feel a draft, there is a plaid throw to cover yourself and logs to be added to the fire. As you warm body and soul by the hearth, flames dance in ever-shifting patterns leading you into a relaxed state of reverie.

Somehow the idea of this cozy countryside home seamlessly works together and brings a sense of calm rather than chaos. I can't say the same for all the patterns I've imagined—or uncovered in the home of my heart and soul.

Notice the Patterns

As you sort through your own clutter, I'm certain you are beginning to see patterns in both your pain and your response to it.

In my personal observing and owning, the Author and Designer of my life has put much emphasis on patterns that pertain to my

- behavior,
- choices,
- habits,
- response and reactions, and
- coping mechanisms.

Patterns in our inner life (as in design) repeat. One flower after the other. One choice after the other. Stripe upon stripe. Pain upon pain.

There is just no getting around it because (remember) "we tend to repeat what we don't repair."[2]

Now that I am aware of the patterns of my soul clutter, some threadbare and clashing, I'm no longer allowed to live on autopilot. Because if I'm the boss of me, I have a say in the direction I'm going. If I'm surrendering and submitting to God and His plan for my life, then I'm participating in the health of my soul rather than continuing to self-sabotage.

Pain is a pattern. When met with the sting of pain, it's our nature to react and cope in familiar ways. Most pain is not original; it's repetitive. Pain may be triggered by different people and instances, but if you look close enough, the trigger is familiar—there is a pattern. Most people have a core wound, an emotional wounding from childhood that accompanies them into their adult life. I once read that a core wound is like a deep pattern in your subconscious mind. I find it helpful to think of it as a lens—a lens through which you see all misgivings and offenses.

I have a propensity to see things through the lens of rejection. I often respond as if I'm being gravely rejected over minor instances. As I mentioned earlier on, if a business proposal or friendly invitation is met with a simple no or "Now is not a good time," it feels personal, and I give way too much thought and energy to the situation. Often we react to a current hurt as if it is the original hurt. As God has helped me to make sense of this deep subconscious pattern in my life, I realized that as a child, I felt flawed.

As you can imagine this also plays out in my marriage and in my parenting. It plays out in every relationship. At times I'm able to use my logical mind and talk myself through the situation, understanding that some things are just a normal part of life (teenagers love you

> Pain may be triggered by different people and instances, but if you look close enough, the trigger is familiar— there is a pattern.

but they say teenage-y things, husbands sometimes have to work late hours, friendships sometimes shift), and other times I circle around a bad pattern.

What does the pattern look like?

- Sting to retreat
- Retreat to self-pity
- Self-pity to a false belief

Or maybe it looks like this?

- Sting to sulk
- Sulk to self-pity
- Self-pity to unhealthy coping mechanism

My pattern of unhealthy coping mechanisms looks something like this:

- Mindless scrolling on Instagram (numbing out)
- Comfort food (a Happy Meal pattern began in childhood)
- Online shopping

These ways of managing or coping with our soul clutter—our pain—end up being detrimental to our emotional freedom. In owning what isn't working, we are free to explore healthy ways to cope, change, and heal.

But how do we own and break a bad pattern?

We look for clarity.

A bad pattern or cycle often comes down to a bad belief. If we want to break the cycle and change the pattern, we have to uncover the bad belief that is hindering us from experiencing joy and living the full life that Christ paid for.

Do any of these bad beliefs sound familiar?

I don't deserve to be happy.
I'll never get over _____.
Things will always be complicated/difficult for me.
I'm not naturally a positive/happy/joyful person.
I'll always carry this pain.
My worry is just concern.
I'm better off alone.
I'm "too much" (too emotional, too sensitive, and so forth) for others.
I'll never be able to afford that, go there, become a _____.

Maybe it's something you've thought. Perhaps it is something someone has said about you or to you. Either way, when we give time and attention to lies, agreements settle in, and they become beliefs.

Look closely at Galatians 5:9: "A little yeast works through the whole batch of dough" (NIV). This means a tiny lie can infiltrate all our beliefs. Once we uncover a bad belief, we need to untangle from it with the truth of God's Word:

I don't deserve to be happy.
    God longs to give me the desires of my heart when I delight in Him (Psalm 37:4).
I'll never get over _____.
    I give my burdens to God, and He will take care of me (Psalm 55:22).
Things will always be complicated/difficult for me.
    God can make a way through the wilderness and rivers in the desert. I won't fixate on old history because God is doing something new (Isaiah 43:16–19).

I'm not naturally a positive/happy/joyful person.

In God's presence there is fullness of joy (Psalm 16:11).

I'll always carry this pain.

God binds up my wounds and heals my broken heart
(Psalm 147:3).

My worry is just concern.

I don't have to be worried or concerned about tomorrow. My
good Father knows what I need, and He will take care of me
(Matthew 6:25–34).

I'm better off alone.

God puts the lonely in families (Psalm 68:6). He goes with
me wherever I go, and He will never leave me or forsake me
(Deuteronomy 31:6).

*I'm "too much" (too emotional, too sensitive, and so forth) for
others.*

I am fearfully and wonderfully made (Psalm 139:14). I'm
learning to walk in love as Christ did (Ephesians 5:1–2).

I'll never be able to afford that, go there, become a _____.

God supplies all my needs according to His riches in glory
(Philippians 4:19).

Design New Patterns

When you become clear of your pattern or bad belief, like me,
confess it and ask God to help you create new patterns—designed
just for you. If, however, you are not clear or can't quite put your
finger on it, pray as David did, asking God to search his heart and
examine him through and through (Psalm 139:23–24).

In taking ownership I'm creating a new pattern. Now when I'm
caught off guard, offended, or hurt, the pattern I'm working with
looks something like this:

- Sting to pray (a simple "Help me, Holy Spirit," muttered under my breath)
- Pray to stay (no more running away, no more hiding)
- Stay to respond (even if the response is "Let's talk about this later")
- Respond to process (acknowledge I'm making progress, notice where there is room for growth)

I mess this up a lot. Sometimes the new pattern mingles with the old. I stay and then I blurt out something rude. I retreat and then I pray. I head to McDonald's and then I process. Rose to rose. Stripe upon stripe. Stay to scroll. Chomping a french fry to crushing bad beliefs. Observe to own to overcome.

Your patterns are not too complicated for God, our great untangler.

CREATE SPACE

Meditate

I am convinced and confident of this very thing, that He who has begun a good work in you will [continue to] perfect and complete it until the day of Christ Jesus [the time of His return].

—PHILIPPIANS 1:6 AMP

Reflect

1. What patterns do you notice in your life? Is there a pattern to how you react or respond?
2. If you were to trace your pattern back to its origin, what would

you find? Can you name a core wound? Does your pattern point
you to any false beliefs?

3. Are you numbing in any way, shape, or form to cope? Do you
   disassociate from difficult situations or decisions?

Act

Make a decision to create a new pattern. Write out how you would like to
respond when met with pain or hurt. Or, map out a response pattern for
when you feel anxiety arising. What healthy coping mechanisms could
you begin to enlist?

16

CONFESS YOUR EXPECTATIONS

There is surely a future hope for you,
and your hope will not be cut off.
—Proverbs 23:18 NIV

Owning my expectations and my disappointment has been the starting point in creating healthy expectations—and finding freedom to hope again and again.

In the midst of my family dynamic changing, I had expectations that some things would stay the same. That people would stay the same. That among the great shift, there would be some familiarity and stability. If every day must be different, then I wanted holidays to stay the same. And when I faced the reality that no, holidays could not stay the same, then I wanted a few traditions to stay the same. These were my expectations—which were usually met with disappointment.

I am not an expert on expectations. As you can see, I'm a fellow traveler working out where I've gone wrong by way of my own debilitating disappointment and conversations with God. I have been lucky enough to have had a few guides—some I know, some I don't. After recounting a situation to my aunt (who's no stranger to uncluttering), she sagely said, "You had expectations." "No, I really didn't," I responded. "Then why the disappointment?" *Gulp*.

One of my favorite teachers, Paul Scanlon, says, "If you don't manage your expectations, you will have to manage your disappointments."[1] I'm now working to manage my expectations like a boss.

Travel Through Your Expectations

When it comes to expectations, we travel through a process with four stages:

1. Having high expectations (idealistic)
2. Lowering expectations (optimistic)
3. Knowing what to expect (realistic)
4. Putting expectations in Christ alone (hopeful)

Our family of origin is the first lens we see through. Is the world our oyster? Is it bright and brimming with potential? Or is it dark, full of setups and systems? Some of us were taught to expect the world, while others learned to expect nothing. In my experience we tend to get way off-balance when it comes to both expectations and disappointment.

I descend from the first camp, and my idealistic expectations only managed to grow to woolly-mammoth proportions that set me up for a steep fall. Life, I learned, has a way of leveling the playing field. When the fall or a leveling occurs, we are swiftly swung to the other end of the spectrum where we are left to live in the land of disappointment. There we spend our time conceiving plans to circumvent further disappointment.

At some point in our lives, hope becomes a risk; it feels dangerous.

In dealing with the unkempt parts of my inner home, I've been making discoveries as God has been uncovering things tucked in the storage tubs of my soul. One thing we've unpacked is that, more times than not in my adult life, my expectation or outlook of the future has been negative. With my mouth I would say that I expect good and believe for the best, because I want to be that kind of person, because I've been raised to believe that words have power, Yet in my heart, He revealed I'm always waiting for the other shoe to drop, for the floor to fall out from under me.

The floor had already fallen out from under me and the climb back up has been long and arduous. *If I don't get my hopes up*, I thought, *the fall wouldn't be so far down.* But the problem is we were designed, created, made to expect much and to expect good. If we are children of God, we haven't just given hope a seat at our table, we've given Him a home in our heart.

> If we are children of God, we haven't just given hope a seat at our table, we've given Him a home in our heart.

This discovery opened the eyes of my heart and I saw that I was participating in self-preservation. Instead of believing, in faith, I put my efforts into avoiding disappointment—even if that meant the self-destructive behavior of disappointing myself before someone else could do it.

Made to Expect

One summer's day, not long after we moved into our new (temporary) home, not long after I launched my first book, I sat outside in the sun and opened my hands, tuning my heart to the voice of Love. It sounds simple and lovely and easy enough, but this was the summer I could barely manage to get out of bed. I was tempted to avoid God, to self-protect from Him. What if He disappointed me too? For me to sit in the sun and open my hands toward heaven cost me something; it was a sacrifice. It was a sacrifice of self—if there was even any part of me left (I wasn't so sure).

Remember the verse—the one you memorized when you were young and full of hope? The one about expectation? The one about your hope not being disappointed? The whisper went.

"Yes," I responded in the language of tears.

I went and found my old Amplified Bible. The one where I first marked the verse in red pen: "Surely there is a future [and a reward], and your hope and expectation will not be cut off" (Proverbs 23:18 AMP). I took those words marked in my Bible, and upon my heart, and wrote them in red on a 3 x 5 index card. And as an act of faith I taped them to the unfamiliar black lacquer fridge in the kitchen, where I'd have to face them every day.

Even though I felt unmoored, there I was, anchored. I've learned that we ought to always pay attention when God says, *Surely.*

How do you self-protect? It seems like a natural enough response. Yet in our attempt to protect ourselves we harm ourselves in the long run. We shut out people, and we shut down potential opportunities. We barricade roads and avenues that are often the very way out and forward.

The question is not whether we will experience disappointment—we will. The question is, in whom or what will we place our hope? A good deal of soul clutter can originate in the expectations we have of others and the hope we put in them.

Maybe the expectations were not even yours in the first place; someone else drew them up for you. Perhaps someone with loving intentions promised you the world. And you believed them, you trusted them. Because why wouldn't you? They had always been good for their word. Putting our expectation—even our hope—in another person usually doesn't happen through a verbal agreement. Usually we don't even realize it has happened until that very important person—a husband, a mother, a father, a friend— disappoints us. Until they can no longer

> A good deal of soul clutter can originate in the expectations we have of others and the hope we put in them.

offer the world, until it all comes crashing down. Sometimes the cracked mirror becomes the clearest reflection because it reveals all the tiny breaks and hairline fractures that were there all along.

The safest place to put our hope is in Christ. That summer when I was at the bottom of the bottom—feeling as if I had lost all hope—Christ remained my anchor of hope. He was anchored to me. There I was, unmoored and anchored simultaneously. Christ is called our living hope. If you don't feel very alive, imagine Him doing the living in you. Not getting our hopes up is not a strategy to avoid disappointment; it's an unhealthy coping mechanism.

I don't know what you are facing. What loss you have experienced. Who has let you down. What you've had to lay down. What gives you reason to feel hopeless. What keeps you up at night and overwhelms you during the day. But God knows. He also knows the dreams and desires of your heart that you've tried to abandon, because they, too, feel risky, like hope. Whether from

> Not getting our hopes up is not a strategy to avoid disappointment; it's an unhealthy coping mechanism.

a long fall from idealistic dreams or a life lived at a baseline of hopelessness—you gave yourself permission not to hope, you agreed to live this way. As I write this, my prayer for you is that today you give yourself permission to hope and believe again.

Our good Father did not design us to live waiting for the other shoe to drop or the floor to fall out from under us. Nor did He design us to put our expectations in other people, in our own plans, or in well-intentioned programs or systems. When we align our thinking with His Word, we are reminded that when our hope is in Christ, our expectation will not be cut off—*surely*.

CREATE SPACE

Meditate

We have this hope as an anchor for the soul, firm and secure.
—HEBREWS 6:19 NIV

Reflect

1. Who or what have you put your hope in?
2. Where are you in the process of expectations (review four stages)?
3. Have you ever wanted God's pity more than you've wanted His freedom or healing?

Act

Write Proverbs 23:18 on a 3 x 5 card or a sticky note. Tape it to your fridge, a mirror, your bedside table, or in your car—somewhere you'll have to face those words every day. Remember, hope is not a risk; it is an anchor.

17

TALK ABOUT THE THINGS

YOU CAN'T TALK ABOUT

If you cannot get rid of the family skeleton, you may as well make it dance.
—George Bernard Shaw[1]

There is an adage in recovery that says, "We are only as sick as our secrets."[2]

Most of us grew up with secrets of some kind—things we knew we shouldn't discuss or things we were told not to talk about. For instance, abuse, addiction, disorders.

Perhaps your secret is that you deal with mental illness or have a mood or eating disorder, something with a stigma attached. We keep these secrets because we are ashamed. We keep these secrets because sometimes they are not our stories to tell. We keep these secrets because we feel isolated and alone. We keep these secrets because we assume that no one will understand or, perhaps, that no one will accept us or the ones that we love. Shame and secrets are like conjoined twins of the soul. It's hard to tell where one ends and the other begins. Which came first. Which is which.

I am not an expert in recovery, but I am well versed in addiction and the destruction it brings. One of my secrets is that addiction runs deep in my family of origin. My grandma Hilda (who, before she died, gave me permission to share her story) was so overcome with shame that she began drinking (which only multiplied the shame).

> Shame and secrets are like conjoined twins of the soul. It's hard to tell where one ends and the other begins.

It was the *Mad Men* era, and my grandfather, a publisher (imagine ones you've seen in movies—sharp in mind and tongue, smoking a cigar), would come home from a long day at the paper and expect her to have a drink with him. The kids were to be fed and put to bed so the adults could have a drink and eat their meal in peace. From what I heard, my grandmother didn't enjoy having a drink. Sadly, their marriage was not a happy one, and after it ended in divorce, my grandma couldn't find her way out from under shame.

Divorce was not prominent in the late 1960s, and in the Dutch Reformed Church it was unacceptable. Chin up—as classy as they come—Grandma held her head high in public. But in private? She couldn't get up off the floor. The shame unmanageable, the emotional pain unbearable. She began to anesthetize with alcohol. She was so private that for years no one even knew she had a problem. In time it could no longer be hidden.

When a person no longer has control over a substance, the substance has control over that person, and there is no hiding, no matter how hard the dependent person tries. After an out-of-state move, my grandma appeared to be in a good place. Enough that my parents put me on a plane at age ten to go visit her in Colorado. But she couldn't stay sober. During my stay, my aunt made a call to my parents that went something like this: "Trina is going to stay at our house. Mom is going into treatment—she's drinking again."

While I was playing store in her basement, my grandma had hit rock bottom. Of course, I had no idea what was happening because it was the 1980s, and adults didn't explain things to children. When I was in my thirties, my grandma told me the story of that visit—the story of her life and how she wanted to end it, and how I played a part, she said, in saving her life.* Her story is one of great pain, hope, healing, and redemption.

Two generations later my sister Amy found herself in unexplainable pain that she didn't know how to communicate, manage, or treat. After growing up with strong Christian values and beliefs, she left our little bubble and dabbled in drugs and alcohol. She was having fun and found it helped numb her pain. I don't mean to make this sound too much like an after-school special, but as many stories go, she thought she was in control of the substance, but instead she had given her power to it. She was also no fool when it came to knowing exactly what kind of destruction and pain addiction brought to both the dependent and their loved ones. She still held her beliefs and values; she knew she wasn't living in the freedom of the cross. This only added to her shame. To the secrets. To the substances. To silence.

I knew she was caught up in some things, but I had no idea

---

* I write in more detail about this in my book *La La Lovely*.

the extent of it. I remember feeling surprised that her addiction was so bad that she needed to go to a month-long treatment program. Under the surface of my surprise, I guess there was shock and denial. *Another person in our family? Where does this stop? When will this end? Not Amy!* Grandma Hilda played a very important part in Amy's recovery. After her own recovery, Grandma Hilda spent twenty-five years leading women in recovery. But it was her greatest joy to help her family. To help those who wanted help. Amy has been sober for seven years. The change I've seen in her, as she's begun to own her soul clutter, has been astounding.

Even on the other side of recovery and with permission to share these stories, I feel like it's a secret I should keep. It feels like betrayal to tell; I feel disloyal. My grandma was proud of her sobriety and recovery, and so is my sister. They, along with my aunt Pat, who has been part of Al-Anon for decades, are the ones who taught me that we are only as sick as our secrets.

I don't know what kind of secrets are cluttering up your soul. But I know they are entangled with shame and deep emotional pain.

When There Is No Closure

A few years ago, near the end of a road trip to Nashville, I happened upon an episode of the *On Being* podcast titled "Navigating Loss Without Closure." Krista Tippett, the host, was interviewing Pauline Boss, author and professor emeritus at the University of Minnesota. Pauline introduced the term *ambiguous loss*, a type of loss in which there is no closure, an incremental death, a chronic grieving.[3] To give you examples, ambiguous loss could pertain to or be the result of things such as divorce, immigration, Alzheimer's disease, or addiction.

Pauline had given language, a term, for what I had been experiencing yet felt I could not explain. Grieving my parents' divorce, the loss of both a home and a person who was still alive—these were all incremental losses. When you bury someone, people come around you and your grief is welcome, it is understood. When there is ambiguous loss—especially when it is a private matter (or one that is secret)—there is no ceremony or ritual that helps bring closure and gathers people around you. Grieving an open-ended loss is confusing enough for the person grieving.

Trust Your Story with Someone

There are people who can be trusted with your story. There are some who will sit shiva with you. Sitting shiva, if you're unfamiliar, is a ritual in the Jewish faith that is practiced after burial and dates back to biblical times. For seven days (*shiva* is the Hebrew word for *seven*) family members sit together to embrace their loss and accept comfort. Many friends come by to share in the remembrance of the loss and to give comfort.[4] *Why don't we see comfort as something that is to be given and accepted?*

The day we finally moved from my beloved childhood home, my friend Erin came over. Erin is a sitting shiva kind of friend. If you have a friend like this, don't ever let them go—they are as rare as a snow leopard. When I was in high school, Erin was my small group leader at church; she's always been a safe someone to share my secrets with. Erin knew the history of my heart and the history of my home. She understood what others didn't, that leaving *that* house was not just packing up, moving out, and moving on. It was more. It was a succinct ending.

Erin came over and said, "We are going to have a ceremony. We are going to bury something in this backyard. We are going to pray and have a service." The loss of the house was very much the last nail in the coffin. A ceremony made sense. So after we walked through the empty rooms, remembering the good and the bad from 1986 to 2018, Erin, my mom, Ella, and I stood under the company of my favorite walnut and Norway spruce trees and dug into the dirt. I placed a few symbolic things representing the greater loss at hand (what and who that house represented to me) in the ground. Then I did my very best to let go. We said, "God, this is Yours, they are Yours, everything always has been Yours. We could not and cannot fix this. Into Your hands we commit this."

We cried and hugged and then hid happy little things in inconspicuous places within the house. (I wonder if the new owners have found my secret somethings.) I didn't want the house to forget me—to forget us. And then it was time to walk out of that grandpa-person-of-a-home for the very last time. My childhood dog, Bobo, is buried in that backyard, along with the tight grip I had around how I wanted my family story to end.

I don't know what you can't talk about. Addiction. Abuse. Disorders. A sibling who is an addict. A loved one who is a narcissist. Estrangement. Hidden abuse. Financial ruin. Perhaps you are grieving someone who is still alive. How do you say goodbye to someone you just said hello to on the phone moments ago? People who sound like themselves in tone, in verbiage, but are no longer themselves. Were they ever who you thought they were? Were there always different personas that you never noticed, put on like a pair of pants, picked in the morning to suit the coming day? Or did they become someone different because the substance, illness, or disorder ate away their identity? "That is not them; that is the substance talking!" my grandma would always say. Could they have just been an idealized personality that you conjured up? A scrapbook character of the past that can no longer be cast in the scene of today. I realize these words might make zero sense to some, but to others, your bones just took a breath. You are missing, grieving, losing someone psychologically.

Dear Reader, some losses linger, and we aren't always promised closure. These heavy secrets cannot be simply filed away, packed up, thrown out, or tied neatly with a bow. We must own the tragedy, the diagnosis, the deep wounds from childhood, the things that we cannot talk about. And the only way to do that is to talk about the things that we cannot, or are afraid to, talk about. When we do this, it brings light into the dark places; it takes the secrets' power away. Hidden things have a way of manifesting outwardly through anxiety and stress.

If you won't talk, your body will begin to talk for you (as we've been discussing). Talking awakens us to the truth that we are not alone—that there are others with very similar circumstances. (Even if your story resembles a Lifetime movie—trust me. People are able to write those crazy story scenarios because something like that happened to someone.) The weight of words we cannot speak is crushing. I'm not suggesting you shout these tender things from the rooftops or talk to just anyone or everyone; that's not wisdom. I'm recommending that you first lay the words at the feet of Jesus. Then talk with a professional—they are bound to confidentiality and equipped to handle the things we cannot talk about. If addiction is part of your story, consider visiting a recovery group or a group for family members of addicts, such as Celebrate Recovery or Al-Anon. Ask the Holy Spirit, our wonderful counselor, to show you how, when, and who to open up to.

Don't let your secrets make you sick. Let the light shine in. Accept comfort. Sit shiva. Surrender whatever it is that your hand has a tight grip on. Move forward, even in uncertainty.

CREATE SPACE

Meditate

"For all that is secret will eventually be brought into the open, and everything that is concealed will be brought to light and made known to all."

—LUKE 8:17 NLT

Reflect

1. Is there something that you "can't talk about"?
2. Have you experienced ambiguous loss? Grief without closure? What has that looked like?
3. Who can you talk to? Who in your life is a sit-shiva friend—who could be? Who can you offer comfort to?

Act

If you've been holding something, if there are words on the tip of your tongue—find a counselor, a trusted friend, or a confidant and share with them.

18

BE AT HOME WITH YOURSELF

The worst loneliness is not to be comfortable with yourself.

—Mark Twain[1]

We've taken ownership and cleared out a lot of clutter. You might not be where you'd like to be, but you're not where you were. Be present in this moment; God is present with you. Accept who you are today; God accepts you. Acceptance isn't an agreement to remain in our current state. It means we welcome ourselves at this stage of our journey. Learn to be at home with yourself, wherever you are, for God is at home with you. He is content living within a home that is under construction, so cozy up and get comfortable too. God does not expect perfection, and neither should you.

This is our reminder that we are on a journey through the hinterlands of our souls. I say "our" because it is my reminder too. Remember, I am a fellow traveler.

It's far too easy to become encumbered with what we uncover, to become completely overwhelmed with all that we are observing and need to own. Therefore, I invite you to observe the progress you've made so far. You're doing the hard work of listening to your pain, accepting a custom plan, paying attention to your body, assessing your emotional age, saying goodbye to comfy and familiar clutter, facing the boxes in the basement, participating in your life, choosing to go through change, imagining space, and enlarging your inner home. You should be so proud. And there's more—you didn't quit! Be encouraged as we look back at all that you've owned: you're telling yourself the truth, embracing mystery, leading your thoughts, declaring your decisions, acknowledging patterns, confessing expectations, admitting the things that you can't talk about, and you are accepting who you are *today*.

> Be present in this moment; God is present with you. Accept who you are today; God accepts you.

Now, let's pause and take some deep, cleansing breaths:

1. Inhale calm. Exhale chaos.
2. Inhale clarity. Exhale clutter.
3. Inhale progress. Exhale perfection.
4. Inhale peace. Exhale overwhelm.

We stand on a bridge called *today*, between what was and what could be. Yesterday is a land some people never learn to leave, and tomorrow is a country we are not yet citizens of. Looking back, as we've seen, has its place in the practice of observation and reflection. Looking ahead, tomorrow can only be seen peering through a lens of worry or wonder, hope or fear, dreams or despair. But today? Today is where our feet touch the ground. It's where we choose to make movement forward or backward. Today is all we really own. We can live but once in today. Today is where we make decisions, take action, love, fail, grow, rest, practice, participate, make progress, change.

And today my prayer for you, Dear Reader, is that you accept yourself right where you are, as you are, in the process. I pray that your lessons from the land of yesterday serve you well, that you see hope in the country of tomorrow and that today you live fully and abundantly.

Will you keep putting one foot in front of the other?

This is the process.

Process is not easy, but it's process that produces results.

You'll fail. You'll get tired. You'll stop. You'll sit. Can you welcome and own this part of the process? There are days when you'll feel like you are going in circles and things look cloudier before they look clearer. Trust the process. There are seasons when we do the right things and don't get the expected results. The process is still working *in you*. I think of the times I've started cleaning out a closet or a storage room, assuming it was a simple afternoon project, only to discover that the quick order I envisioned had turned my home into an even bigger wreck—everything out in the open, appearing to take up even more space. Many times we can't even know what we need until we get into it. Do we need more time? More supplies? A rest? Perhaps more help? It's at these points that we yield to overwhelm or make the choice to continue on and overcome.

Take heart because God knows, and He is right in the thick of

> Yesterday is a land some people never learn to leave, and tomorrow is a country we are not yet citizens of.

it with you. And at some point He will begin to reveal the purpose of the process. Being faithful to proceed in the process always bears fruit.

In my own process to be at home with myself—to own my self-worth—God kept me circling around Psalm 139. I was at a point of feeling the conflict of wanting desperately to be seen and wanting to hide my nakedness.

> You have searched me, LORD,
>   and you know me.
> You know when I sit and when I rise;
>   you perceive my thoughts from afar.
> You discern my going out and my lying down;
>   you are familiar with all my ways.
> Before a word is on my tongue
>   you, LORD, know it completely.
> You hem me in behind and before,
>   and you lay your hand upon me.
> Such knowledge is too wonderful for me,
>   too lofty for me to attain.
>
> —Psalm 139:1–6 NIV

It was as if I was at a rest stop gaining an understanding of how God perceives (He discerns, distinguishes, observes, regards, feels, senses, is aware of) every moment of my heart and soul (mind, will, and emotions). He knows every step we will take before our journey even begins. He's behind us and already ahead of us. Can you feel the peace? I can. The pressure is off you. The pressure is off me. This is the gospel—it is not our work, it is His. You are known, accepted, and loved as you are on the way to becoming who God created you to be. And He's made the way—He is the Way.

Let's continue our journey, then.

CREATE SPACE

Meditate

Read Psalm 139.

Reflect

1. How are you finding yourself in the process? How are you feeling at this juncture of the journey?
2. What progress (no matter how small) are you proud of?
3. Are you starting to notice purpose in your process? What are you noticing?

Act

Take a moment to close your eyes and envision this journey that you are on. See yourself putting one foot in front of the other. Take in the scenery—beautiful or untidy. Notice how far you have come. How much more space you have created. Notice that you have not been uncluttering alone—God's strong and kind presence is with you. Conclude by taking four deep, cleansing breaths:

1. Inhale calm. Exhale chaos.
2. Inhale clarity. Exhale clutter.
3. Inhale progress. Exhale perfection.
4. Inhale peace. Exhale overwhelm.

Part three
Overcome

Once, in a tight place, you gave me room.

—Psalm 4:1

19

TELL YOURSELF A NEW STORY

The soul becomes dyed with the color of its thoughts.
—Marcus Aurelius[1]

W e all tell ourselves stories. About ourselves; our lives; our pasts, presents, and futures. We return to stories of past traumas, old wounds, stressful situations. We replay hurts, grievances, and past history. We paint vivid imagery in our minds of what could potentially go wrong. We build stories, carry on conversations with characters in our drama, and create scenarios that will likely never play out. We author a narrative within. A living script, if you will, that winds and flows like a river throughout our day, colored with characters that come in and out of our story, their own narratives mingling with ours, sometimes building a dam and making a home in our soul.

A story I tend to tell myself doesn't start with *once upon a time*. It begins, *I'm so tired*.

Some mornings feel like a million pounds on top of me. They feel new and hopeful—and as if they were not made for me. I feel like morning's prisoner. Her snow-globe cellmate. I smell possibility. I hear it in the chirp of the birds and the rustling of the leaves. I see it in the sunlight shadows shimmering from the sky down to the green grass. I feel its mobility in the free-flowing breeze. It's all light. It's all airy. Why, oh why, am I so weighted? It is the kind of day when going to the grocery store seems like it will be an impossible chore—the deciding more than the doing. Some days I don't know what to do down to the dinners, the chicken, the green beans.

I am tired before I wake. I am tired before my feet hit the ground. *I am so tired*.

This is a story I tell myself.

It's not a story without fact. All stories, even fiction, even lies, dabble in truth. The truth is, I am not a high-energy person. I'm just not. Even when I do all the right things. But what kind of story am I truly telling? Perhaps this next story is a familiar one to you too.

There must be something wrong with me. I am missing something. Did I lose it along the way?

No, I think it was something I never fully possessed. Something I can't purchase. Something I can't fake—for long. I am not interesting enough. I am not beautiful enough. I am not fun enough. I am not smart enough. I am not confident enough. I am not lovable enough.

I scarcely embody these attributes, but it is not enough. For them. For me. I am not good *enough*.

This is a story I tell myself. The truth is, *enough* is an ending that fits wherever I fall short. What kind of story is that?

When we moved out of our house, I told myself I may never have a home that I loved again. I dabbled in the business of lowering my expectations to get a return of no disappointment.

The Characters and the Script

The thing about our stories (the ones we tell ourselves, the ones we relive, the ones we project) is that they are our stories, our plots. But our stories, even the ones in our heads that no one will ever hear, are never entirely of our own making. The characters have a story of their own going, and the role you play in their story may not match the part you play in yours (and vice versa). Think about it.

I recently heard a podcast where a therapist, Esther Perel, explained this, saying: "The story of a relationship, it's not just the story you tell yourself, because the story you tell yourself is influenced by the character that you have become in other people's stories." She went further by explaining, "You have been recruited for a play in this relationship that you never auditioned for. You become a character in their plot."[2]

> Our stories, even the ones in our heads that no one will ever hear, are never entirely of our own making.

I had to ask myself, *How has the projection (real or perceived) of another person I'm in a relationship with affected me?*

What about you? Have you fallen into a role that someone else cast for you? Good sister. Bad friend. Perfect son. Nagging wife. Unstable spouse. Stubborn child. Stern father. Boring housewife. Overachiever. Abuser. Manipulative. Overbearing. Cold.

Is there a story that someone is telling about you? How does it align with your narrative? All the bells rang for me when Esther said, "The story is never created by one person, it's a co-creation."[3]

We must also ask what role have we assigned for ourselves? Perfectionist? Worrier? Lost cause? Workaholic? Addict? Victim? Loser? Boring? Worthless?

What are your stories?

What are your roles?

Speak to Your Soul

The great thing about a story is that you can always begin a new one. You can stop returning to worn-out stories and tragic chapters. You can choose to use your imagination to reframe a situation and dream up new possibilities—to envision God's promises in Technicolor. You can always tell yourself a new story. Your character can develop. Your plot can twist. The role you've been assigned in someone else's story is not your assignment.

I start new stories by speaking. *Why?* Because usually there is a narrative that needs interrupting. As we know, it is important to pay attention to the soundtrack of our soul, but to overcome we need to speak to our souls—to give a new line, a new direction, to reframe. Our mind and emotions love to be the star of the show, but at some point, if we want to overcome, our will must take the lead.

In Psalm 42 David gave us the script on speaking to our souls (or pouring out our souls). He started by acknowledging his heartbroken soul. He inquired further, asking his soul,

> Why are you in despair . . . ?
> And why have you become so restless and disturbed
>   within me?

He then carried on, telling his soul what to do:

> Hope in God and wait expectantly for Him, for I shall again
> praise Him
> For the help of his presence.

He continued to speak to his soul, saying,

> Yet the LORD will command His lovingkindness in the
> daytime,
> And in the night His song will be with me.
>
> —vv. 5, 8 AMP

The trajectory of my story is changing as I speak to my soul. When I feel the familiar heaviness of depression, I use David's prayer in Psalm 42. When I fall short and find myself back in one of my many "not enough" chapters, I speak Psalm 139 and I practice listing in my journal things that I like about myself and the person I am becoming (overcoming is a process).

When I am tired in body or soul, I speak 2 Corinthians 12:10—and remember that my weakness attracts God's strength. When I catch myself lingering in yesterday, I remember and speak Isaiah 43:19—God is doing a new thing. *Don't you see it?* He asks. "Yes," I answer.

> Hope in God and wait expectantly for Him, for I shall again praise Him / for the help of his presence.

And I'd let myself imagine. I'd envision a new home—beautiful and beloved. When I began doing this, as soon as I'd start, I'd stop to self-protect. When I realized I was self-protecting, I spoke the words taped to my fridge: "There is surely a future hope for you, and your hope will not be cut off" (Proverbs 23:18 NIV).

Speaking to your soul is one of the most powerful ways to not only unpack your soul clutter but to get it out of the house. Some stories are dated just like your grandparents' tattered old chair, your old concert T-shirts, or trinkets from childhood.

We live in a day and age when everyone is finding, professing, and confessing *their* truth. My truths (whatever they may be) shift and change, which is why there must be *a* truth. I am interested in taking what I think to be true and holding it up to the light of God's unchanging Word—*the truth.*

In unpacking my stories and holding them up to the light, I'm learning to reframe and reroute storylines. Narratives that seem harmless are anything but if they hold us back. It's good to ask ourselves, *Is this story propelling me toward the person that I want to become or holding me hostage to a version of myself that is no longer relevant?* It is our choice to break free from that kind of clutter and overcome.

In this final section we'll continue to unpack ways to practically overcome. We discuss tools for living an emotionally free and spacious life. As you consider these practices and take action, I invite you to continually shift your focus from hard work and hustle to receiving and yielding.

Overcoming Made Easy

I find that there are two ways to view overcoming.

First and most importantly, we must understand that *we are already* overcomers. The pressure is off. It's not on you. You don't achieve the status of overcomer by hustling and striving to overcome every obstacle by your own grit and determination (thank God). If you are a child of God, then you *already are* an overcomer. First John 5:4 tells us that our faith is the victorious power that triumphs over the world. Once we have an understanding of who we are in Christ, we can begin to overcome what has been overwhelming us.

Once we have an understanding of who we are in Christ, we can begin to overcome what has been overwhelming us.

We are overcomers.

Second, overcoming is something that we do—it's not an elusive arrival; it's participation with the Spirit. It's ongoing-ness. We can practice overcoming. We practice being who we are.

As I studied the word *overcome*, it reminded me of the other way we use the word: "She was overcome with grief." "He was overcome with joy." *Overcome* also means an overwhelm of emotion. In fact, one way that *Merriam-Webster* defines *overcome* is simply "overwhelm."⁴ These two words, *overcome* and *overwhelm*, seem to hold hands.

Imagine overcoming your soul clutter (emotional pain, fear, anxiety, depression) by being overwhelmed with peace and joy! This is the new story we are going to tell ourselves. We are overcomers! We are overcoming! We are overwhelmed with peace and joy!

CREATE SPACE

Meditate

This is what GOD says,
　　the God who builds a road right through the
　　　　ocean,
　　who carves a path through pounding waves,
The God who summons horses and chariots and
　　armies—

> they lie down and then can't get up;
> they're snuffed out like so many candles:
> "Forget about what's happened;
> don't keep going over old history.
> Be alert, be present. I'm about to do something
> brand-new.
> It's bursting out! Don't you see it?"
> —Isaiah 43:16–19

Reflect

1. What are some of your stories? What lines do you repeat in your mind like a mantra? Like a soothing insult? What past experiences keep showing up in today?
2. Who are you giving too much headspace to? Has someone else assigned a role for you? Has their narrative seeped over into yours?
3. Do you have a propensity to try to overcome in your own strength? How can you yield to the Spirit in your everyday life?

Act

Write out your storylines for clarity. Then seek out a scripture that you can use to speak to your soul. Feel free to start with Psalm 42.

20

TAKE YOUR POWER BACK

———

You can be pitiful or powerful, but you cannot be both.
—Joyce Meyer[1]

It was just after Christmas, and Stephen had been given a book called *Keep Your Love On* by Danny Silk. I flipped through it because . . . books! I didn't fan many pages before I made a hard stop on a chapter titled "Powerful People, Powerful Relationships." In the chapter, Silk describes the difference between powerless and powerful people. Have you ever had one of those odd moments where you simultaneously cringe and celebrate? A heavenly machination of sorts. This was it for me. There was no doubt that I was living like a powerless person—*cringe*. And there was no doubt that I was ready (by the Holy Spirit's leading and by the choice of my will) to do the work to start living like a powerful person—celebrate!

I was confused and conflicted, because in my own understanding I would have never identified as a powerless person. I knew my identity in Christ was that of an overcomer and a victor. Also, I'm a highly responsible person. Yet the situations I was dealing with left me feeling helpless and like a victim. On top of that, people I viewed as powerful people were losing their power. I even watched some willingly give their power away. It's astounding how crisis, change, and hardships reveal who we really are and what we truly believe.

Whether I had the wrong idea of what a powerful person was, or I took on a victim identity in difficult situations, or I perpetuated a mindset of helplessness because I felt helpless—here I was. I was exactly as Silk describes: "Because they cannot take responsibility for their decisions, powerless people are relegated to reacting to whatever is going on around them on a daily basis."[2]

The question wasn't whether I was a responsible person; the answer was I didn't even make decisions because all my energy (mental and physical) was used up reacting to everyone and everything around me. I also had to come to terms with the fact that I had given my power away to other people, as well as to a mindset.

"But as a powerful person," Silk juxtaposes, "I do not simply react to whatever is happening today. I am able to take responsibility for my decisions and the consequences of those decisions—even for my mistakes and failures." He continues with this phrase, which has become a mantra of mine: "I can *respond* today and *create* my tomorrows."[3]

Becoming a powerful person sounds rather glamorous and impressive, but in reality it looks a lot like muddy underground growth, like organizing junk drawers. I realized that my definition and perception of a powerful person was skewed. I was ill informed. Maybe you were too? Perhaps this concept is fresh and new information for you right now in this moment. A powerful person is not someone who demands respect and makes commands. A powerful person gives respect and takes command of his or her own life (choices, attitudes, and decisions).

While we can willingly give our power away, there are also times when people will try to take your power. Maybe it seems as if some have already succeeded in doing so. The good news is that you get the final say; you can take your power back. It's important to know that anyone who tries to take someone else's power is not a powerful person. They are simply a bully trying to attain power by control and manipulation. This can be as subtle as someone testing your boundaries or someone criticizing you because you have boundaries. There are those that demand to be in charge, deeming themselves the authority. And there are others who are sly and cunning. They pretend to have your best interest in mind, bloviate of their so-called sacrifice, and make you beholden to them. It isn't always easy to spot or untangle from them.

> A powerful person is not someone who demands respect and makes commands. A powerful person gives respect and takes command of his or her own life (choices, attitudes, and decisions).

But what about when we give our power away?

Sometimes we hand it off like a baton, like a gift, like a box to a salvage shop.

With a feeling of obligation.
With the sign of a paper.
With the hope for peace.

With a drink from the bottle.
With the hunger for love.

The phrase "owning your power" is often used in recovery programs. Author and codependency expert Melody Beattie often talks about this as knowing the difference between feeling victimized and being victimized as well as removing oneself as the victim.[4] Beattie says, "By owning our power we don't have to become aggressive or controlling. We don't have to discount others. But we don't discount ourselves either."[5]

I wonder in which ways may we be discounting ourselves.

I had been reading about a father in the Bible who brought his possessed son to Jesus for healing. The father said, "If you can do anything, take pity on us and help us." "'If you can'?" Jesus replied. "Everything is possible for one who believes." The father responded, "I do believe; *help me overcome my unbelief*!" (Mark 9:22–24 NIV, emphasis mine).

I realize that in the above text, "take pity" is likely to mean "have mercy on us"—but it got me thinking about how many times I had been coming to God in need of a healing, yet what I kept expecting from Him was pity. We want God's pity for our situation, but God wants to give us freedom and bring change to our circumstances—He needs us to believe.

What or who have you given power to? We can also interchange the word *power* with *space*.

Who is taking up too much space in your mind, in your soul? What is taking up too much space?

Here are some things we can give our power to:

Other people
Money

Substances
Approval
Disparaging words
Success

A few ways we can begin to take our power back:

Establish boundaries
Practice responding instead of reacting
Forgive (others and yourself)
Take responsibility for (own) your choices
Create a healthy distance from toxicity
Seek help or treatment if necessary
Give more attention to solutions than the problem
Build your confidence and don't attach your self-worth to other people

Taking your power back begins with a decision, sometimes involves repentance, and always requires choice upon choice. Don't worry about getting it wrong or not having the proper supplies. You already have what you need—*God has given you a spirit of power,* love, and a sound mind. Things are looking more spacious already.

CREATE SPACE

Meditate

For God has not given us a spirit of fear, but of power and of love and of a sound mind.

—2 TIMOTHY 1:7 NKJV

Overcome

Reflect

1. Would you consider yourself a powerless or powerful person? Be honest.
2. Where or how have you felt helpless or powerless? Why?
3. In what ways can you begin to live like a powerful person? How can you turn your focus onto taking command of your own life?

Act

Pray this prayer:

Lord, I thank You that I have not been given a spirit of fear but of power, love, and a sound mind. Uncover the areas in my life where I am feeling victimized or have been a victim. Thank You for healing my wounded soul; I want to begin to live powerfully, starting today. Amen.

21

TRUST GOD WITH YOUR TIME

*One theory I find rather comforting is that time
exists so that everything doesn't happen at once.*
—Madeleine L'Engle[1]

I am not a patient person. This will show if you ask me to paint straight lines along trim or ice a cake. It will show around 8:30 p.m., when it's nearly the children's bedtime, and in February when a Midwest winter is at its worst.

I am not a patient person, but I have learned to wait. In fact, I feel like I've been living in a perpetual holding pattern.

For me, I've waited on the following:

- a move
- answers

- others (will they choose change?)
- professional opportunities
- healing
- relational dynamics (will they progress or digress?)
- God's provision
- a new day
- a pandemic to end

I imagine you have a waiting list of your own.

In early December of 2018, I escaped my waiting place with my mom and children as we traveled to 1930s London by way of *Mary Poppins Returns* on the big screen. I left my worries in trade of wonder.

The lights dimmed; I clutched my popcorn and Milk Duds and sighed with anticipation of the practically perfect in every way Mary Poppins. Not only would this movie transport me and widen my wonder, I was certain that there would be some clue or more likely direct proverbial wisdom from the stern yet sugary-sweet nanny who always knows just what to do.

And then the movie began with these words projected upon the big screen: "The Great Slump."

I turned to my mom and said, "Yes, the Great Slump." We shared a knowing. We shared a familial Great Slump.

Slump means "to sink into a muddy place."[2]

The Great Slump, I learned, was another name for the Great Depression (leave it to the Brits to make it sound more interesting, like a story rather than a diagnosis).

The Great Slump gave a name to a decade of my life.

The year that was coming to an end marked climbing out of an epic bog: losing grandparents, leaving my beloved home, an estranged relationship, launching a book, settling into a temporary home, heightened anxiety, deep depression, Ella switching schools, and attempting to begin again in the same town, in the same place, in a feeling of muck.

In *Mary Poppins Returns*, Michael Banks (now grown), along with his children, is faced with leaving their beloved home on Cherry Tree Lane. Times are hard, life has been unkind, and the bank—the one his father once worked at—is now in a place to repossess it. The irony and unfairness was as thick as the London fog.

When the house is finally empty and they are all saying their goodbyes, Michael chokes out: "Goodbye, old friend." Clearly, I am not the only one who understands a home to be a friend. I choked up too.

Now, of course, this was a movie (a Disney movie!), and they were able to save their old-friend-of-a-home at the second strike of midnight (because they turned back time—because Mary Poppins is magic). Mary and Burt didn't show up in my story. But the truth was, as much as I did not want to leave my home, even a second stroke of midnight could not change that it was time to go. I knew in my bones that I had to not only move out but, most importantly, move on.

Change is a tricky thing; it's both a tortoise and a hare. Slow and swift. It's both a long time coming and happens in an instant. It's the growing into it that takes time. When my unmooring (what I call the move from my childhood home) took place, I deceived myself into believing that things would change in an instant. There was such an extreme buildup to a moment marked by a moving truck. "You might be surprised at how good you feel when you leave that

> Change is a tricky thing; it's both a tortoise and a hare. Slow and swift. It's both a long time coming and happens in an instant. It's the growing into it that takes time.

house," friends would say. Supercalifragilisticexpialidocious. I wanted it all to be movie magic, but it wasn't. Some things can be right yet still feel sad or confusing.

I would now be waiting for the change in me.

Waiting Is Active

The Bible is story upon story of waiting, of individuals who—before they saw victory or freedom—spent time waiting on the Lord.

- Abraham waited to be a father.
- Noah waited for the rain to start and then for it to stop.
- Joseph waited for his dream to come to pass.
- Esther waited to have an audience with the king.
- Job waited for his suffering to end.
- David waited to be king.
- Mary waited for the birth of her Savior son.

Most of the waiting places were far from glamorous:

- In the belly of a whale
- In the desert
- On an ark
- In a cave
- In a pit
- At the tomb

An indicator of our soul's health is our ability to keep in step with the Spirit. Isaiah 40:31 reminds us that waiting on the Lord renews our strength. Likewise, a soul that is becoming healthy does not rush out ahead, nor is it in a hurry. Surrendering our timeline is active participation.

Micah, who waited for God's justice, said, "But me, I'm not giving up. I'm sticking around to see what GOD will do. I'm waiting for God to make things right. I'm counting on God to listen to me" (Micah 7:7).

Psalm 27:14 encourages us to "wait for and confidently expect the LORD" (AMP).

Active waiting looks different for everyone. That is why we must not compare our waiting with another's or judge someone else's journey. In Esther's waiting she spent a year beautifying herself. In Noah's waiting he spent decades building an ark. In Joseph's waiting he advised a country. In David's waiting he was on the run. In Jonah's waiting he was sitting in the dark among whale excrement.

Waiting may feel unfair—someone else's choices may very well have brought you to a waiting place, as Saul did to David, as Joseph's brothers did to him. Waiting may make you feel ashamed, because your own bad choice brought you here (cue Jonah). Waiting may make you question God's promise and tempt you to take matters into your own hands as Abraham did. God was taking too long so Abraham ensured a son by way of a concubine. We all know the trouble that caused, not only within his family but also with nations.

> Active waiting looks different for everyone. That is why we must not compare our waiting with another's or judge someone else's journey.

God is faithful to His promise. He was faithful to Joseph and David who did nothing wrong. He was faithful to Jonah and Abraham who made bad choices. God will be faithful; it's who He is.

I've found active waiting is a tug-of-war of the soul. My way. God's way. My timing. God's timing. My work. God's work. My plan. God's promise. The sooner we let go of the rope, the sooner we are able to stand up and follow.

Don't be in a hurry. Overcoming is a process. Lasting change takes time. There will be days when you begin to question what it is you are even waiting for. Keep on. At times you'll mistake God for slow. Keep on. He is never slow and always thorough. Other times, you'll want to take matters into your own hands. Remember Abraham. Keep on.

The Invitation of Stillness

When you feel stuck in the waiting, look for the invitation.

A surprising thing that I've learned about *stuck*—whether it is literal or hypothetical—is that it always comes with an invitation. Stuck asks if we'd like to meet stillness. It's a quiet whisper of an invite, so quiet most people miss it. And it's confusing because it's easy to believe that stuck is a brute and a bully forcing stillness, unsuspectingly, on those who were just trying to live their lives.

But perhaps we'd be wrong to believe that stillness can be forced. Can you force a child to sit still? You can bribe them with ice cream or, perhaps, a consequence for momentary compliance, but ultimately, they must choose by an act of their will. Stillness cannot be forced; it can only be chosen.

I wonder if you've recognized how some welcome stillness while others fight it? Stillness is uncomfortable because it reveals what we have been avoiding, ignoring, and anesthetizing. It reveals our hopes, fears, and motivations. It reveals behavior, habits, clutter, and coping mechanisms. It calls us to keep company with our truest selves. Stillness, I believe, is anything but stuck because it creates movement in us. It moves us forward in a way that striving never could. It clarifies what had been confounding us, before we were ever confined, and how to move beyond.

In fact, in our waiting and stillness we will be prompted to act. To move on, move out, move forward. In these tucked up, tight places, God gives us hope and reveals dreams, visions, and plans. Our impulse will be to act. We've felt stuck, cramped up with our clutter for so long. Our souls are now experiencing movement, and we want our lives to follow.

But before we get ahead of our-selves, ahead of God, remember that the interior movement is of far greater importance and always a precursor to exterior movement. Sometimes we simply need to stay with ourselves before we take a step. But make no doubt, God wants us to take steps—this is how He directs us (Proverbs 16:9).

> Stillness . . . moves us forward in a way that striving never could.

I don't know where you have felt stuck, why or how life has felt on hold for you, but God knows. And I've felt it in my own life, at times so acutely that I wasn't sure if rolling into a new day really made any difference. I felt it living in my hometown and childhood home, my life seeming to repeat my parents'. I felt it with the impending and uncertain move out of my home. I've felt it in battling depression (stuck personified). I've felt it in relational patterns in my marriage, spinning around and around. I've felt it living in a temporary place. *How long will we be here? Will we buy a home again? Will it be in this town? Will we move away and have a fresh start?*

In my temporary home, the Lord in His kindness taught me to be still—to choose stillness. All of me was worn down. I was weary from sorting through my clutter—no matter how many corners I'd turn, there was more. I could see the new square footage and an open floor plan full of potential; I just could not get there. I was ready for growth and for change, but God had me stay. Not to stay in my clutter—rather in the stillness. There were yet things that needed to be revealed.

Knowing When the Time Is Right

In my stillness I read a story in the Old Testament about Isaac. He experienced a terrible famine in the land and wanted to *go*. Isaac had a plan to escape to Egypt. But God stopped him and said, "Don't go down to Egypt; *stay where I tell you*. Stay here in this land and I'll be with you and bless you" (Genesis 26:2, emphasis mine). Isaac stayed put. This was enough of a full-stop moment for me, as running was my escape of choice when feeling stuck. A new place, a new town, a new beginning to wrap up my endings—it sounded ideal. But what I began to understand, through Isaac's life, is that the blessing isn't connected to where we go; it's connected to our obedience and God's presence.

Stay put; I'll be with you.

Because of Isaac's obedience, he was so blessed in his work that the king wanted him to leave (Genesis 26:16). So Isaac left and returned to the wells that his father Abraham had built. He began to dig them up, only to find that his enemies had clogged them with dirt. It seems he did his own uncluttering by digging and clearing wells. After dealing with opposition, he eventually was met with "wide-open spaces." In fact, that is exactly what the name of his final well, Rehoboth, means. He said, "Now GOD has given us plenty of space to spread out" (Genesis 26:22).

Do you see this?

My heart skipped a beat when I read those words, when I saw that stuck and struggle were not the antithesis of space—they were part of the process. God was not trying to hold Isaac back, constrict or constrain him. He was creating space. In the end Isaac made a covenant of peace with the king.

There was space for peace.

Observe with me the progression of this story because I see it as a map:

Obey ⟶ Stay

Be blessed

Go ⟿ Battles.
(deal with opposition)

Wide-open spaces ⟿ Peace
(with enemies)

To get to the wide-open space in our soul, we, too, must journey through some of these very same things, through some of these very same places. Whatever God tells us to do, we must do it—stay, go, obey, battle, dig in the dirt. The blessing and the wide-open space—the clutter-free soul—isn't an arrival; it is a place accessed through obedience and the presence of God.

About a month after studying Isaac's story, we were given the opportunity to go. Stephen was interviewing for a job in a state that we had been talking about moving to for years. A place we drove through yearly, and often when we did, I'd hear a whisper: *One day you'll live here.* It was so quiet and so private; I didn't dare tell a soul. We were almost freaked out by this opportunity. The timing felt a little off as our daughter was going into her junior year of high school. We weren't yet ready to buy a home. But we explored the opportunity anyway because we both believed God gave us this open door, and we knew deep down, at some point, we were likely to go. There was a lot of thought, prayer, and counsel that went into our decision. It was difficult to conclude that this wasn't right—because we really thought it was.

> The blessing and the wide-open space—the clutter-free soul—isn't an arrival; it is a place accessed through obedience and the presence of God.

We stayed.

In years past I would have felt this immense disappointment. Likely so heavy that I would have taken on a new layer of stuck. There was some disappointment, but I realized that this exploration of an opportunity also came with a choice. God was not teasing or tricking us. He was nudging us forward. Would we take a step? He, then, directed those steps. To the natural eye it may have appeared that we only traveled in a circle, ending up right back where we started. But that simply wasn't the case. There was movement in our souls—expansion—that no doubt will give guidance to a future *go*.

I always find it good to remember that God is not in a hurry with me; I don't need to be in a hurry either. It's His work to get me unstuck; it's my work to choose to trust Him with my time. And anyway, we miss too much in the hurry. Dear Reader, the genesis of creation and growth begins in the dark and in the dirt.

CREATE SPACE

Meditate

"The LORD is my portion," says my soul,
"Therefore I hope in Him!"

The LORD is good to those who wait for Him,
To the soul who seeks Him.
It is good that one should hope and wait quietly
For the salvation of the LORD.
                    —Lamentations 3:24–26 NKJV

Reflect

1. Are you in a season of waiting? What are you waiting on?
2. Are you afraid of stillness? What part? Would you be willing to accept the invitation to get still?
3. Ask God what He would reveal in the stillness. What might God be asking of you in this moment (obey, stay, go, battle)?

Act

Practice waiting. Here are a few ways you can do that:

- Continue to participate in your life—don't stop living.
- Take time to sit in God's presence to listen and observe.
- Journal/write down anything and everything you are learning.
- Read the Bible. Study those who waited on a promise.
- Surround yourself with friends who can see where you're headed—even when you can't.

Overcome

- Hope and dream anyway. Don't believe the lie that you'll be disappointed.
- Take steps toward the future you are waiting for.
- Surrender as many times as you must, embracing mystery.

22

PURSUE PEACE

———

The ability to simplify means to eliminate the
unnecessary so that the necessary can speak.
—Hans Hofmann[1]

I t was the last day of 2019. After all the holiday hullabaloo, my
family and I boarded a plane to Florida to celebrate the New
Year and vacation with lifelong friends. The warm air was such a
welcome; we were all happy to escape the brutal cold for a week. As
I settled into vacation mode, exhaling the breath I had been holding
all through the holidays, I made a decision to take a break from
social media. My body felt almost resurrected by the sunlight and
lack of schedule, and I knew my soul needed new life too. To fully
relax into a rhythm of laughter and lightheartedness I had to make

a choice to be fully present. Just as I had to get on an airplane to a physical place of rest, I had to get off the phone to get to a mental place of rest.

The week went on, and we visited our favorite beach on Captiva Island, ate as much seafood as we possibly could, had meaningful conversations, picked up pickleball in the mornings, laughed a lot, and saw colorful sunsets . . . and I didn't post one picture to show for it. At first, I felt the itch, like a leg covered in mosquito bites. There were so many pretty things to share—palm trees, sunsets, pastel houses, an entire shore of shells, food that everyone probably couldn't care less I was eating. There were memories I wanted to chronicle and share—playing pickleball like old people, our kids all ages and stages playing together at the beach, eating ice cream outside and bike riding in January, all images of what decades of friendship and vacationing together looks like.

After the initial itch subsided, I found that I was quite content to snap these memories to my phone and keep them for myself. It turns out we don't have to share every thought, moment, or memory with the entire world. And in many ways this made our time together on this trip more precious.

When I returned back to the Chicago cold, my body tensed up. But my mind, my soul, seemed to have more space. I liked this new feeling. This foreign, winter feeling. Suddenly the winter blues didn't seem as blue. The day didn't seem so scattered. My brain didn't seem so cluttered. I found clarity by not crowding my day, and my life, with everyone else's. I didn't have to take on everyone else's thoughts, ideas, opinions, agendas, or offenses. I only had to deal with my own. And that was much easier to do when not muddled with the masses. I slept better. I had more focus. I gave more attention to people face-to-face. It felt really good. Like freedom. Like peace.

I returned to Instagram because I left without notice and because it is part of the work that I do. I do love connecting with people and encouraging them, and this medium has worked for me. However, what I've learned over time and with observation is that when social media begins to work against us, it's time to reassess or take a break. We have the choice; we can pursue peace.

> When social media begins to work against us, it's time to reassess or take a break.

Take a look at Psalm 34:14: "Seek, inquire for, and *crave peace* and *pursue (go after) it!*" (AMPC, emphasis mine). It's a good thing to crave peace, but we can't just want it and wish for it; we have to pursue it—to look for it and inquire for it.

How do we do this? How do we pursue peace?

First, I think it is most important to remember that peace has already been given to us (John 14:27), and if we are in Christ, then the Prince of Peace lives within. Peace is at home with us. This kind of peace can never be taken from us. It's the peace that believers find themselves enveloped within during the most distressing of times. This is not the type of peace we can strive for; it is the one we receive and rest in.

The peace that we can pursue is a peace we can partner in. We can take responsibility and own the choices that have kept peace at bay. We can overcome by making room for peace and taking action to welcome it within our lives.

Get Practical with Peace

There are many practical ways we can pursue peace, but I want us to begin by looking at two approaches.

Input Versus Output

We live in a world of uninterrupted input. Think about this with me: 24/7 news, one thousand friends at our fingertips, podcasts in our ears, pundits—professional and not—pontificating, meetings about our meetings, books, articles, Netflix, family on Facebook, recipes to try, DIY projects to add to the list, products to purchase, advertising chasing us down, what "they" said, what we perceive "they" didn't say, unsolicited advice, other people's struggles—on top of our own. And the list could go on. Even music—although wonderful—is input.

Now consider what forms of output you have. What is your ratio of input versus output, production versus consumption?

I am a high-input person. Much by choice, much by design. Years ago I took the StrengthsFinder Personality Assessment and learned that one of my strengths was called Input. My coach explained that people who score high on input have a need to collect things: information, ideas, artifacts, even relationships. What I acquire, even if just information or ideas, is worth compiling and storing because I might find this information useful or worth sharing at some point (great, I'm basically a hoarder of ideas). When I learned of my input strength, I was blogging, and it was actually quite perfect because that was my output. I gathered words and beauty, and then I shared.

Intentional output is one way that I pursue peace. For me this looks like writing (even if just in my journal), walking, getting out of my head and into my body, creating (using my hands), and connecting with others—face-to-face.

In her book *The Next Right Thing*, Emily P. Freeman talks about being a "soul minimalist." I like this word picture because not only is it about uncluttering our souls—getting rid of what is holding us back—it also speaks to being conscious of what we allow in. Emily says, "Becoming a soul minimalist does not mean that you should hold on to nothing but rather that nothing should have a hold on you."[2]

Being mindful of my input is another way I pursue peace. I choose where and who my input comes from. Instagram, not this month. Doom scrolling, not today. Family drama, not at the start of my day. The news, not before I go to sleep.

Often we are listening and seeking answers from everyone and anyone but God and ourselves. I hope you've accepted the invitation of stillness, that you choose it because, as we learned in the last chapter, stillness reveals. And one of the greatest gifts that stillness reveals is God's voice—and our own.

I know what you are thinking. Stillness either sounds amazing, terrifying, or impractical. I understand, but what I can tell you is that it is achievable. *When we put ourselves in the way of peace, we are met with it.* Stillness is one way that I put myself in the way of peace. In the early hours of the morning I am met with quiet. It's a sacrifice to wake before the sun, but the return is far greater than the invest-

> Often we are listening and seeking answers from everyone and anyone but God and ourselves.

ment. In this hour I can hear only the crackle of the fire and the cadence of my thoughts. I sort through them as they come, like laundry—dark and light—and I lay them out before God. I ask, "What would you say to me?" And then I listen. I write what I hear, what I feel—the dark and light. I read the Word—a sure way to hear; it's the first input I desire for my day. In an oxymoron of a move, I then seek stillness through gentle movement. Moving my body by stretching or walking (barefoot on the grass, crunching the leaves or snow underfoot) stills my mind.

I find peace by igniting the senses. Lighting a candle and pausing to watch the flame flicker as I breathe in the citrus scent—appreciating a whiff of summer in the dead of winter—before I move on to my work. Opening the patio door, taking a small step outside—no matter how cold—to gather fresh air in my lungs. With every inhale I take in peace, and with each exhale I release the stagnant mental clutter of my subconscious. I choose peace by stopping the scroll and looking out my window—taking in all the shapes and colors found nowhere else but in nature. In moments like these—and they needn't be too long—I hear my own needs and desires and I hear the voice of Love leading me.

More or Less

Years ago I wrote a blog post on the idea of "more or less." It's never difficult to focus on what needs fixing, where we are lacking, or what we need to eliminate from our clutter. But what about what we need more of in our lives? Naming these things takes intentional introspection. Could more of the right thing crowd out the wrong? I believe so. I found that more or less was a way to pursue peace—to seek and inquire about the things I want more of in my life, and to help eliminate the things I don't want (peace stealers).

The following is my More or Less List that I wrote at the beginning of 2020, while on my two-month-long Instagram break. I hope it helps you think about things you may need more or less of.

- More IRL (in real life) conversations and experiences
- Less Instagram/phone/digital living
- More encouragement
- Less criticizing and correcting
- More nourishing foods
- Less emotional eating

- More love
- Less fear
- More joy
- Less sadness
- More laughing
- Less crying
- More trusting
- Less self-protection
- More risk
- Less playing not to lose
- More stories
- Less drama
- More generosity
- Less withholding

I encourage you to pursue peace and keep putting yourself in its path. It takes practice, and sometimes it takes getting used to. Peace can feel strange and boring when you are addicted to drama, constant input, and the low hum of chaos. Sometimes our souls need a detox, and detoxing is never comfortable. Yet it is a way for us to overcome and move forward.

CREATE SPACE

Meditate

The mind governed by the flesh is death, but the mind governed by the Spirit is life and peace.

—ROMANS 8:6 NIV

Overcome

Reflect

1. Are you overwhelmed with input? What forms of input could you eliminate or cut back on?
2. Who or what has the greatest input in your life?
3. How can you personally pursue peace and practice stillness?

Act

Where do you need focus and freedom? Think about this and create your own More or Less List.

23

ENGAGE TO FIND A BETTER WAY

*Thought is an amazing thing; it can be a mirror, a
lens, a bridge, a wall, a window, a ladder, or a house.*
—John O'Donohue[1]

W hen we know only one way, that's the way that we take.
Even when the old way of doing things just isn't working.
I remember attempting to clean out our playroom. I was armed
and ready with black garbage bags, a giveaway box, and energy from
a McDonald's Coke. I marched down the stairs, with my kiddies
following close behind, and straight into the playroom, which no
longer appeared to have a floor. I began holding up toys and stuffed
animals one by one, demanding a consensus from my four children.

"Oh, I love that toy. I forgot about that! Keep it!" "I know what
that little piece goes to—save it." "I'm gonna take that one up to my

room." Then they'd come across a like-brand-new, squidgy stuffed animal and say, "Get rid of it."

That's when I'd chime in, "No, you can't get rid of that. It's a Jellycat. Remember, Gommy bought that for your birthday. I love that one. It's too cute not to keep."

Our way wasn't working. I needed a better way. So I asked my friend Kendell (the expert) to help. She began by having the kids separate the items into categories, setting a timer, and then giving them simple choices. "You can keep three stuffed animals," she said and set her timer (she may have also made me leave the room). She kept the kids from overthinking, redirected when necessary, and showed us all a better way.

Not only did I have to find a better way to unclutter the playroom, I also had to learn a better way to deal with my emotions.

"How are you?" my sister checks in.

"I'm Candy Crush."

For a season, Candy Crush wasn't just a game I played, it was a mood. This mood had the look of me sitting on the closet floor, blue light glassing over my eyes. This mood had the sound of a finger *tap, tap, tapping* and sometimes tears *splat, splat, splatting* on the screen. The mood carried too many thoughts to make sense of in words. Not even my writing seemed to help, so I crushed candy. I crushed my way to level 432. I crushed my wild-eyed emotions into a blue-screen blank stare.

"I'm Candy Crush" meant I couldn't quite articulate how I felt, but also that I didn't want to. It was code for "I don't want to get into it right now, Amy," or "Oh, you know . . ." This code never needed deciphering because we were sorting through the same familial clutter.

You might understand this mood if you've ever felt like life is just *too* much. The ends. The waiting for change. The betrayals. The confusion of a conversation. The abandonment. The intentional pain someone causes. The deception. The schemes of others to take what is not theirs. The sickness. The bewilderment. The digging for truth.

I was just beginning to learn about my emotional health in the early candy-crushing days—I was not to the point of owning or overcoming my soul clutter, but I was paying close attention. And it was clear that I was having trouble regulating my emotions. The clarity eventually allowed me to own this long-lived pattern and take responsibility for changing it. Spiraling and crushing candy were getting me nowhere.

Get Practical with Your Soul

Our souls are made for wonder. Passionate. Artistic. Childlike. Romantic. Circular. Ethereal. Flowing. Wild. At least, I like to view my soul as such. I don't imagine it rigid, businesslike, square, boring, or regimented. My soul speaks in colors, shapes, places, and poetry. In freedom and play. My soul sings in the wide-open places (take me to Colorado and I come alive).

While I believe we were made for wonder and wide-open spaces, our souls are not exempt from practicality. The necessity of clearing out clutter is what gives us clarity and insight on how to create the space we long for.

We can learn to be practical with our souls. If the soul is a compilation of the mind, will, and emotions, then we must evoke the obstinacy of our will and the logic of our mind to work for us, rather than against us—no matter what our emotions may have to say about it. In this way, we overcome.

While I believe we were made for wonder and wide-open spaces, our souls are not exempt from practicality.

When my children were younger and acting out, I tried to help redirect their frustration and roaring emotions by playing a made-up game called "Better Way." I'd start by saying, "Let's play a game." This shifted the atmosphere. "Rocco says you hit him because you wanted that toy," I'd say. "Rocco started it; he took Giraffe," Liam would wail. Instead of scolding, I would ask, "What is a better way? If you didn't want Rocco to take your toy, what is a 'better way' to tell him?"

Of course, this didn't always work, and as they get older, they roll their eyes and laugh at me for my made-up games and sayings, but it did always work in the sense that it got them thinking about an alternate way to respond and behave. It helped them come to their own conclusion, even if they were not ready to admit that their behavior or reaction was not working for them.

This is not so different from how the Holy Spirit teaches me. Yet another reminder that our wondrous souls need continual parenting. In the safety of unconditional love, we are able to be honest with ourselves and look for a better way.

In the presence of unconditional love, I admitted that I needed a better way. My emotions had to be hushed, my mind engaged—seeking the patterns, repetition, and results (and lack thereof)—and my will commissioned to repent.

Yes, repent. The Greek word for *repent*, *metanoeó*, means "to change one's mind or purpose," to "change the inner man."[2]

Regulate, Don't Ruminate

To change my mind, to find the better way, I had to first look at the data. The data was clear in revealing that when I'm met with stress or overwhelmed by something, my repeated response was one of the following:

1. Freak out / meltdown (emotional outburst)
2. Talk about it, think about it, talk about it (ruminate)
3. Candy Crush or closet (distract)

And if the analytics of my soul revealed one thing, it was that my repeat offender is rumination.

I come from a long line of ruminators. We are professional "talk about it, think about it" talkers. We analyze, cross-examine, and then talk things into the ground. And in a family where there has been a lot of drama, there is *always* something to "talk about, think about, talk about." If we are not talking about it, you can bet your bottom dollar we are thinking about it. What he said. What she said. What they meant. Responding in my head or out loud in the shower (come on, I know I'm not the only one). Going over all possibilities and scenarios. (Disclaimer: I'm all for processing, and some of us are verbal processors. But I'm learning the difference between healthy processing and rumination.)

The better way I'm working toward is *equanimity*. It's a word that kept chasing me around in books and on podcasts and paper. Equanimity is "mental calmness, composure, and evenness of temper—especially in a difficult situation."[3] It's my new code word of sorts that evokes a gentle reminder that I can choose a better way.

The choice is mine.

The choice is yours.

No matter our reaction of habit, when we are met with stress and negative emotions, there are practical fixes we can engage to grow in equanimity. In her book *Stress Proof*, author and doctor Mithu Storoni tells us,

Becoming better at self-control and self-regulation can help you control negative emotions when they are ignited. Those who have good self-control tend to cope better with stress. . . . A healthy brain will usually use a combination of strategies to regulate emotion.[4]

Did you notice the word *strategy*? It's key because I think we must get businesslike with the emotional side of our brain.

Like Dr. Caroline Leaf, Storoni also shares research that points to the conclusion that redirecting our thoughts and creating new ones can rewire our brains. "Over time, an overactive emotional brain has trouble bouncing back," she says. "If you get into a habit of recognizing a negative thought, detaching from it, and actively switching your attention to something positive or natural, your world will change."[5]

> No matter our reaction of habit, when we are met with stress and negative emotions, there are practical fixes we can engage to grow in equanimity.

Our worlds do change, for better or worse, based upon the habits we employ. It was clear that I needed to switch my habit of freak out, talk about it, Candy Crush it, to something else:

1. Recognize (observe!)
2. Detach
3. Switch attention

"Once your negative emotions overwhelm your mind, it becomes difficult to evict them. Your rational brain needs less strength to *prevent* entry than it does to carry out an *eviction*."[6]

I love the imagery Storoni gives, as it coincides with the heart and soul as a home. Our uncluttering work is the work of eviction, yes. This makes great sense as the process of "rumination" is also called "dwelling."[7] Why would I want to give residence, a dwelling place, to emotions that cause chronic stress and make it difficult for my brain to bounce back? Catching the clutter upon entry is an eviction warning to the clutter that's long been squatting on your soul. It's killing two birds with one stone; it's a one-two punch.

Stress Proof shares an array of both short-term and long-term fixes to regulate negative emotions and cope with stress (I highly recommend getting a copy of the book). As I read, I was surprised to find that, in my own way, I was attempting to regulate.

My habit of endlessly scrolling Instagram when stressed or upset was a subconscious attempt to detach. I didn't have it right, however, because Instagram engages the emotional brain. How many times has your scroll led you to feeling not enough, jealous, insecure, lonely, frustrated, left out, unhappy, scared (thank you media), confused, or angry (thank you politicians)? I'm going to guess *every time!* Unless you are lucky enough (or excellent at curating your feed) to be met only with beautiful inspiration (remember when that's all Instagram was in the beginning?), encouragement, and laughter (if it wasn't for the memes that cause laughter).

What I was getting right, without knowing the science behind it, was the concept of looking for beauty. By noticing beauty in the everyday (this is the premise of my first book), I was practicing switching my attention. And, as it turns out, crushing candy wasn't just an escape either. Candy Crush engaged my rational brain.

I read of a small, controlled study in which volunteers were made to feel sad. (How, you ask? By recalling sad memories and listening to melancholy music. Sounds like a typical day for an Enneagram Four.) Then they did a working memory task, such as play *Tetris*. The brain scan of those who participated in the working memory task showed the brain's suppressed emotional reactivity and reduced activity in the amygdala.[8] You can bet I've dusted off my 1989 Nintendo skills and now use *Tetris* (as well as word games) to help me regulate my emotions. Rather than a Candy Crush closet shutdown, I now use a brain game to bridge. I break reactivity and rumination by intentionally engaging my rational brain (and my will) and then practice returning to the next thing. The goal now is not to escape but to engage.

We can also employ other tools that will help the stress and overwhelming emotions to pass through, rather than take up residence:

- physical activity
- focused work: work that you lose yourself in—for me this is writing
- real-life community
- breath prayers: an inhale and exhale followed by a short prayer

When I was in the throes of depression, my breath prayer was "Let light shine out of darkness" (2 Corinthians 4:6 ESV).

I am finding a better way, and I believe you can too.

For a list of my favorite breath prayers, visit
trinamcneilly.com/breathprayers

CREATE SPACE

Meditate

Fix your thoughts on what is true, and honorable, and right, and pure, and lovely, and admirable. Think about things that are excellent and worthy of praise.

—PHILIPPIANS 4:8 NLT

Reflect

1. How do you react when met with stress or overwhelm? Do you notice a pattern?
2. Do you ruminate on negative emotions or situations? Be intellectually honest.
3. Do you need to repent?

Act

Download a brain game on a device (my favorites are *Tetris*, Word Trip, and Wordscapes in Bloom) and try using it to engage your rational brain and switch your attention. Tip: Use this tool as a bridge by setting a timer for five to ten minutes. When the timer is up, engage and get on with your day.

24

NURTURE AND NOURISH

*My friend . . . care for your psyche . . . know
thyself, for once we know ourselves, we may learn
how to care for ourselves.*
—Socrates[1]

It's a skin-stinging eighteen degrees outside today, and I just returned from a walk. I'm from the Midwest and we are hardy people; my blood runs thick like maple syrup (that's "seeer-uppp"). My tolerance (don't confuse this for affection) of frigid weather is far superior to that of my husband, who is from the South. However, I shouldn't gloat because his tolerance of heat and humidity is one I'll never understand. I'm no wimp when it comes to winter, but it still takes an act of the will to bundle up like Ralphie from *A Christmas Story* and head out to walk in weather that catches your breath and freezes your nostril hairs.

In years past I reserved my winter walking for the treadmill, but these days I'm compelled to get outside. The fresh air clears my mind. The wind whooshes away the stale thoughts sitting heavy on my brain, like wet towels before the spin cycle. Breathing in fresh air opens the window of our souls. Stale air out; fresh air in. Thoughts that have been stuck move along. Ideas that couldn't quite form begin to take shape.

In the Netherlands this wind walking has a name. It's called *uitwaaien* (oiut-vway-ehn), and Dutch people have been doing it for over a hundred years. *Uitwaaien* is one of those cool words that has no English equivalent, but it best translates to "outblowing" and is akin to spending time in the wind. It's what the Dutch do to clear their minds—they go out into nature to walk, to ride bikes.[2] They intentionally walk into the wind.

I've long admired, and watched from afar, the European lifestyle of walking and riding bikes everywhere, every day. For them, walking is not exercise, it is movement from here to there. And weather, although something to complain about, is not a deterrent.

Why can't I walk in the rain? I began to ask myself. The British do.

It's the Swedes who shifted my mindset entirely. They live by the Scandinavian concept of *friluftsliv*, which translates to "open-air living." The Nordic countries have a motto: "There is no such thing as bad weather, only bad clothes."[3] You'd think in the colder climates we'd be suited with proper clothing, and you'd probably be right. We are, but we don't often wear them. "I don't need a coat, I'm just going from the house to the car," we say. In fact, I've given up making my children wear a proper coat to school (unless it's above twenty-two degrees and I know they will be playing outside); their blood is maple-syrup thick too.

I started wearing proper clothes for the cold and getting outside. And every time that I do, without fail, my cluttered head clears. It doesn't have to be long; sometimes it's truly so cold that I can only withstand ten to fifteen minutes before a head-clearing turns into a headache. It's never so much about keeping the clock; it's more about forgetting there is one. *Uitwaaien*, I read, comes from the concept of replacing "bad air" with "good air."[4] And that is what I do on these walks.

My friend Leah walks every day—"unless it's raining sideways," she says. I like that. I always spy her at drop-off, parking her car on the outskirts of the parking lot. In our town you can't walk everywhere, but Leah creates little walks throughout her day wherever she goes.

One of the best ways to sort through internal clutter is anything but mental; it's physical. Getting out of our heads and into our bodies is not only a good place to begin, but it's also a practice we can return to every day. Many of us have become completely out of touch with our own bodies. Some of us even live inactively in our bodies and overactively in our minds. I find that life is almost too cerebral these days with the insatiable hunger for and exposure to endless information. Our spirits and bodies need equal attention.

> One of the best ways to sort through internal clutter is anything but mental; it's physical.

I'd like to outline three familiar yet important areas of health, that if given proper attention, will help us create space for more peace and joy.

Movement

It's likely we're familiar with studies and research that outline the many benefits of exercise. We've long known that cardio workouts are good for the heart. And we are all learning just how much of an effect exercise has on our mental health—boosting our mood by releasing endorphins. Exercise is no longer just for trying to look good. Movement is now for feeling good. Our bodies work in conjunction with our souls, and thus nurturing our bodies will have a profound effect on our minds, wills, and emotions. No two bodies are the same, and we have to treat them as different (when it comes to exercise, when it comes to food).

The greatest hack I've discovered about movement is this: you will do it if you like it. I've always been drawn to gentler forms of exercise: walking, Pilates, yoga, aerobics, light weightlifting. I don't like to sweat. I'm not very competitive. And I really don't like going to the gym.

When I was a teenager, I tuned in to ESPN every day to work out with Denise Austin. I was a cheerleader at the time, and I suppose I liked jumping around and doing routines. A few years ago I began following Denise on Instagram and decided to join one of her summer fitness challenges. I was surprised at how much I was looking forward to exercising each day, not just because it was nostalgic. I liked it because, apparently, I still liked jumping around. Surprisingly, I don't even mind breaking a sweat when I'm doing something I enjoy.

I discovered how effective getting my heart rate up and breaking a sweat (even just a small one) was in clearing the mental clutter. I also noticed that Denise's signature upbeat, encouraging, smiley style had a huge effect on me. I was in desperate need of encouragement, and it turned out even someone on a screen smiling at me, saying things like "I believe in you" and "Let me see that beautiful smile" and "Make today a great day" had the power to make a difference in my soul (remember, words have power). It finally made sense why I shied away from intense classes with intense, kick-your-butt instructors. I thought it was because I didn't want to push myself, but it turns out I didn't want a stranger yelling at me, and I didn't care to compete with the person next to me.

I've never wanted to go to spin class because of those two reasons. I only kind of wanted to go to see what all the fuss was about. Several of my friends love spin. During my summer of Denise, I was visiting Mindi—a spin-loving friend—in Colorado, and she convinced me to go to a class with her. Guess what? I didn't like it (I should note that the instructor was not mean—intense, but not mean). And I felt okay about it. Mindi loves spin—and that's great. She is competitive and energetic and an extrovert. The camaraderie and competition are a good fit for her.

I'm quite consistent with exercise because I feel better when I do it. I want to take care of my body; I have to do it for my mental health. These days, however, I prefer to call it movement. I'm not interested in keeping time or tracking steps or calories burned. I'm simply keen to make sure I'm getting enough movement each and every day. I've found that a simple five-minute stretch first thing in the morning has almost the same feel-good effect as twenty minutes.

There are a few things I am strategic about and do routinely, but I also allow myself freedom to flow with what my body feels like or needs on that day or in that season. At the onset of the pandemic and lockdowns, I did aerobics or Pilates in the morning and then took a walk in the afternoon, sometimes finishing my day with stretching. When mental clutter is at a maximum, I find I need more movement. Fortunately I've learned a few things about movement:

1. Walking is for everyone.
2. Do what you loved to do as a kid.
3. It's not about how long; it's about how often.

Sleep

We all love sleep, except when we aren't getting it. If you are a new parent, you know exactly what I'm talking about. You know that feeling of living encumbered in a groggy cloud that you can't seem to step out of. Everything and everyone is "extra."

Sleep is restorative to both our minds and our bodies. It's when our organs are at work, as well as our brain, sorting, storing, and repairing. Our brain and body intuitively know how to unclutter and do so while we sleep.

When I don't get enough sleep, I often feel like I'm carrying the day before into the next, and when it compounds into weeks or months, well, it's hard to stand up under it. I've had years where I wasn't sleeping well because of colicky babies, stress, and choice. Yes, choice. When my babies did finally begin to sleep, I used their sleep-time as "me time." I would stay up until the wee hours of the morning working and blogging. I enjoyed it, but I didn't realize until years later, when I started going to bed at a normal time, how much that had a terrible effect on me. No wonder I was so crabby all the time and so low on energy. When I don't get enough sleep now, that crabby character returns, and I've identified her as the sleepless monster.

I'm older now; I cannot work until two in the morning, and I no longer want to. Yet there are some nights in which I simply cannot sleep or find myself waking up around 3:00 a.m. Sleep can be a sneaky fair-weather friend. Thus, I find creating an inviting environment for sleep helps. The experts call this "sleep hygiene." Things like making sure your room is dark, your mattress is comfortable, and abiding by a bedtime routine really can make a difference. I'm not perfect with my bedtime routine—I think it matters more to have one and do it sometimes than not have one at all.

The following is my sleep routine (not necessarily in order):

- stop scrolling an hour before bed (this is the goal)
- a hot Epsom-salt bath
- a cup of tea (decaf, of course; my favorites are chamomile, Sleepytime, and peppermint)
- stretching
- reading
- watching a comedy (I know TV is a blue light, but I love laughing before I go to sleep)
- melatonin if needed
- pray/talk to God as I try to fall asleep

Food

Nourishing our bodies with good food and nutrition is another way we can care for our souls. Food is very personal. We all have specific feelings about food. Some of us are great at nourishing our bodies, while some of us punish our bodies. What we believe about food and what we put into our mouths impacts our mental health as well as our bodies.

I am not a dietitian or professional. I can only share my personal experience with food. I would like to tell you that I follow a particular eating plan that has changed my life and promise that it will work for every one of you. But I've tried several methods over the years, from a twenty-one-day vegan program to Paleo, and I've bought more programs than I've followed through on. I love the knowledge; I'm not always so great at implementing all the input.

In my research and experimentation, what I've concluded is that there is not one particular plan that has worked for me. I have had to alter my diet many times, based upon the needs of my body in different seasons.

At the very end of my twenties, I lost twenty pounds following the *French Women Don't Get Fat* method. I learned so much about portion control. I ate on a smaller plate, I stopped mindless eating, I walked thirty minutes every day without fail (there's that European walking thing again), and I learned to make trade-offs (I want the chocolate more than the chips).

In my thirties I went gluten-, dairy-, and caffeine-free and also tried a vegan diet. I learned I could live without dairy but not without bread. I also discovered that my body does not digest beans well and that I need more protein.

In my forties (where I am now), I've dabbled in intermittent fasting (feeling the benefits of giving my body ample time to rest and digest) and am focusing on intuitive eating and low-inflammation foods.

I don't eat perfectly. I aim to eat well 80 percent of the time and have my treats 20 percent of the time. I'm a girl who still loves to get a Happy Meal. However, I've observed that when I'm not doing well emotionally or I'm under stress, I tend to go straight for the bad stuff—for comfort food. It's taken me a long time to admit that when I'm feeling bad, I don't take care of myself. This is when I'm prone to eat poorly. Yet when our minds are overwhelmed, our bodies need nurturing and nutrient-dense food the most.

There is no doubt that the foods we eat affect how we feel. According to Harvard, "Multiple studies have found a correlation between a diet high in refined sugars and impaired brain function—and even a worsening of symptoms of mood disorders, such as depression."[5]

Growing up, I watched my dad eat a lot of seafood, which was pretty rare in the '80s when you're landlocked in the middle of the country. Every time he ate salmon he would say, "Fish is brain food." While we all rolled our eyes and laughed, we learned to love fish (in fact, if my family had a mascot restaurant in those days, it would have been Red Lobster).

Over the years my dad continued on with his brain food, eating pickled herring from a jar and taking teaspoons of cod liver oil. Of course, I thought that might be taking it too far, but he was onto something. Research confirms that fish high in omega-3 fatty acids are excellent for our brains. Now I cook salmon, or some sort of fish, every week, and of course my kids roll their eyes and say, "Gross! Not again!" I just laugh and say, "Fish is brain food."

Dr. Amen, author of *Change Your Brain, Change Your Life*, points out how foods work for us or against us, stating that "the foods you eat can either fire up overactivity in your brain's limbic system (emotional center), which brain scans show is linked to depression, or it can calm activity to promote more positive moods."[6] Often we are contributing to the mental clutter simply by the foods that we eat. (That's a truth I need to let sink in.)

I understand that eliminating foods (that taste so good) is overwhelming. That's why I find it helpful to begin by adding good foods. Recently my friend Abby reminded me of the "add in" approach, which I used to follow. More of the good stuff makes less room for the bad. Why not try adding more mood-boosting foods? A few that Dr. Amen recommends, to get you started with reducing depression and boosting your mood, are berries, water, lean protein, salmon, kimchi, saffron, avocados, and dark leafy greens.[7] Having an all-or-nothing mentality has never done me any favors.

I think it's important to remember that God is interested in the nourishing of our bodies as well as our souls. He created the two to work in conjunction. An unhealthy body makes for an unhealthy soul, and an unhealthy soul makes for an unhealthy body. There is no doubt that the work we are doing to unclutter our souls will have a positive effect on our bodies. Furthermore, nurturing and caring for our bodies will help to bring healing and health to our souls.

There is a Bible story I read about as a child in which the prophet Elijah called down fire from heaven. He wanted to show the people who the one true God was. Elijah also saw the skies open with rain, which he had prayed for after three years of drought. Then after Elijah experienced a major victory, Jezebel (the evil queen) threatened his life. Even with God's provision of victory, Elijah became so afraid, felt fear to such an extreme, he ran from the queen's threats and hid. But he didn't stop there. He was so exhausted he told God he wanted to die. Elijah did what we all do when depleted and depressed—he went to sleep.

> An unhealthy body makes for an unhealthy soul, and an unhealthy soul makes for an unhealthy body.

God responded by sending an angel to give Elijah food, drink, and a nap. Elijah ate the meal, then went back to sleep. The angel of the Lord came back with even more food, and before long Elijah was nourished enough to walk forty days and nights to the mountain of God—when he got there, he crawled into a cave and went to sleep. It was there that God spoke to him. He simply asked Elijah, "What are you doing here?"

After Elijah went through his diatribe of "I've been working my heart out for you, everyone has abandoned your covenant, I'm the only one left, and now they want to kill me," God told him to go stand on the mountain and that He would pass by. First, a mighty wind went by; then an earthquake shook the earth. Next, a fire roared, and then came a gentle and quiet whisper. The gentle, quiet whisper of God asked Elijah the same question, and again he moaned. God responded kindly, telling him in great detail what to do next.[8]

Wherever and however you find yourself, God knows what you need next—a nourishing meal, sleep, a walk, a retreat. God refreshes tired souls *and* bodies (Jeremiah 31:25), and I believe we can partner with Him by minding our health through movement, sleep, and nourishment. In doing so, you'll feel freer and lighter, as if the window of your soul has been opened to let in the fresh air.

For my morning movement video, visit
trinamcneilly.com/morningmovement

CREATE SPACE

Meditate

A sound mind makes for a robust body,
but runaway emotions corrode the bones.
—Proverbs 14:30

Reflect

1. Are you inactive in body and overly active in mind? What small changes can you make to create a shift?
2. What type of movement do you enjoy? How does your body like to move?
3. What is your relationship with food? Are you giving your body nutrients and nourishment?

4. Are you getting enough sleep? What is hindering you from the sleep you need?

Act

1. Try *uitwaaien*. Take a walk in the wind.
2. Add three nourishing foods into your meals this week.
3. Create a bedtime routine.

25

ASK FOR HELP

"Asking for help isn't giving up," said the horse.
"It's refusing to give up."
—Charlie Mackesy[1]

I don't know what ideas you have about help and asking for it, but I can be sure you have opinions. We all do. And many of them stem from childhood and what we absorbed in our upbringing.

I grew up in a home that, by today's standards, would be categorized as privileged. My father owned a successful business and work was his focus. He didn't fix things around the house or mow the lawn; he hired people to do that. My mom was a stay-at-home mom who worked various jobs throughout the years. We had babysitters and cleaning help. It seemed there was always someone at our house fixing, repairing, or updating something.

My maternal grandparents were helpers. They lived two hours away, but whenever they came for a visit they helped, whether it was painting a room, putting toys together on Christmas, or watching us kids so my parents could take a trip. My grandma was an extreme helper. It was not unusual for my mom, as a teenager, to come home to find that her mother had brought home a stranger to eat with them or live in their home for a season. She would literally give people the clothes off her back.

My father was accustomed to hiring help because his parents did so. His father was a prominent publisher, and his mother was also involved in the business, which often demanded she entertain executives. I don't want to paint an inaccurate picture here. These were hardworking people. My grandfather began working as a child, not long after his own father put him in an orphanage. His work as a paperboy in Canada cost him part of his fingers from frostbite while delivering newspapers during the bitter winters. They worked hard and hired help as needed. Both my grandmother and dad knew their strengths—which were cerebral—and that is where they put their efforts and energy.

As I look back, both of my parents have been helpers. Both exemplified extreme generosity—sometimes to a fault. My dad might not have been one to help someone build something with his hands, but he helped with his checkbook. My mom gave her time serving in the local church. She still gives her time helping with her grandkids, volunteering, and leading Bible studies. She has always been exceptionally generous with her time and her pocketbook. You cannot leave her house without her giving you something. Often her last words as you're leaving her house (after "I love you") are "Take it! Take it!" When I was a child it was normal to see my parents giving things away right out of our house.

Conversely, I come from a long line of people who didn't ask for help when it came to emotional needs or support. Both sides of my family had their own version of what I call the "ups": pull *up* your bootstraps, chin *up*, put *up*, grow *up*, cowboy *up*.

This is my history of help. And, in general, I don't like to ask others for help. I'm comfortable helping others, paying for help (if it's within my budget), and depending upon family for help.

As things began to fall apart in my life and there was a need for help, I didn't want to seek it out or ask for it.

> *I didn't want to ask for help because I thought I should be able to muster up the strength to deal with things (I should just try harder). After all, it was my mess. My clutter.*
> *I didn't want to ask for help because I didn't want to be an imposition. I didn't want to put anyone out. I didn't want anyone to feel obligated.*
> *I didn't want to ask for help because I didn't want anyone to know the extent of my situation.*
> *I didn't want to ask for help because I believed I couldn't afford it.*
> *I didn't want to ask for help because I could not handle rejection.*
> *I didn't want to ask for help because I was supposed to be the one helping others.*
> *I didn't want to ask for help because, quite simply, it's uncomfortable.*

All these reasons, I can see now, are colored in shame, false humility, and pride.

And all these reasons are excuses.

When my mom finally convinced my grandpa to move closer to family, she was left to clean out a home filled with seventy-seven years' worth of life. She couldn't do it alone, so my cousin, Nicole, and I helped. Physically cleaning out three stories (plus a packed garage . . . yes, this was the grandma with *the* basement) and sorting through three generations of memories couldn't be, and shouldn't be, done alone.

When it was time to leave my home, the preparation felt like an impossible project. There was the emotion of it, which often left me feeling debilitated, and then there was the physical work, which felt impossible under the emotion. This home had several generations' worth of things packed into the belly of it. Of course, my mom helped in every way that she could, but she, too, was preparing to leave her home at the time. It was all too much. We both needed the help.

Sometimes you pray for help, sometimes you pay for help, and sometimes you ask for help. Sometimes you do all three. Papa Roy and Grandma Evelyn (family friends that we've adopted as our grandparents) helped us with an enormous garage sale. My sister-in-law Lindsay was there too—she sat with me and made me laugh as I sold furniture, and memories, I wasn't ready to part with. She sat in shock with me when a scrap metal truck showed up, and a shirtless guy jumped out to throw my kids' old bikes and other pieces into the back of his truck. I teared up thinking of how he was going to melt down memories, but Lindsay had me laughing and noticing the comedy (the kind you couldn't write if you tried).

> Sometimes you pray for help, sometimes you pay for help, and sometimes you ask for help. Sometimes you do all three.

On the last day of the garage sale, my friends Jen and Jer showed up with pizza and the kind of laughter that can only come from lifelong memories. My friend Kendell was there every step of the way. She is an organizational wizard and a strong worker. I wasn't in a good place to make decisions, and she knew just what to do with everything. I was happy to hire her to help us.

On one of our last nights in the house, my friends Liz, Lisa, Jenny, Anna-Lisa, and Lori all showed up for a dance party. Lori made me a flower crown and Lisa gave me a Disney Princess scepter.

The only thing that remained in our 1976 sunken living room was a disco ball. Together we danced our hearts out and my tears away. These friends showed up to help me celebrate "what was" and the promise of a new beginning.

Just the other day I was wringing my hands, completely overwhelmed with a relationship that needed mending. I was supposed to be writing, but the soul clutter of this strained relationship was fogging up my mind, clouding my words. The emotional pain became physical; the worry turned to anger and tears. I climbed up the spiral staircase of the loft I was working in, and looking out to the skyline, I cried out to God for help.

How many times has the only prayer I could muster been *Help!?* Too many to count. In this past decade I have come to know the Holy Spirit as my Helper (as He is so aptly called), and the words of Isaiah 41 as my daily bread. I've also come to understand that my help-prayer carries a tune of "Rescue me!" It is the cry of my heart. Yet it is my soul that turns it into a wish. A wish that echoes "Make it all go away." I have known God to miraculously rescue, but what I'm finding in this uncluttering business is that His help—His rescue—has looked a lot like Him teaching me to help myself. The Way showing me the way.

On this particular day, I was desperate for a word, a sign, even a distraction from myself. In the little space atop the staircase there happened to be two books propped on the little potting shelf next to me. One was a biography and the other a little gift book about heroes of the faith in the great cloud of witness. I flipped through the gift book only to stumble upon a chapter about Nehemiah. In this familiar story I recognized something new: Nehemiah had to ask for help. He was broken over the destruction that had come to his city, his home, which was no longer safe. In grief over the ruins he prayed to God (a beautiful reminder that He is, indeed, our first and best source for help), and God answered by leading

Nehemiah to ask for help. He asked the king for aid, and he also asked the people to help him rebuild.

In that moment, looking out at the small-town skyline, I knew I had a choice. I could either continue to spiral out of control emotionally, or I could choose to practice what I'm preaching and take ownership. In my owning up I realized that overcoming would entail asking for help. "We should ask others for help when the problem is bigger than us and when we face opposition," the gift book read.[2] I knew I had to make an appointment with my counselor. The problem was bigger than me. The situation that needed mending was way out of my league. I not only needed expertise, I needed support. Before I could begin listing all my "up" idioms, I booked an appointment. And then I booked a bunch more.

I wonder what you might need help with. What are you trying to solve, sort, or carry on your own? What reasons might you have for not wanting to ask for help? What are your excuses?

Whatever your reasons, it's important to lay them out. There was a season when I would say, "I can't afford counseling." If you had looked at my bank account, you would have agreed. But as I began to recognize that everything is a choice, I had to realize that how I spent money was also a choice. If I would have cut back on eating out, or not taken a trip that year, there would have been money. The truth I had to own up to was that I didn't want to prioritize counseling with my money.

In every moment that I have had help (whether paid for or not), I've found myself feeling not so alone in what felt like solitary work. The thing is, you are the main character—the leading role—in your soul, but you are not the only character. Many people have played a part in cluttering your soul, and many will play a part in helping you unclutter your soul—if you will allow. As my sister says, "Help is about someone seeing you." The Enemy of our souls wants us to believe that we are alone—in every way. We become discouraged with thoughts like, *You can't ever tell anyone what was done to you; they won't believe you, and they won't accept you. You got yourself into this mess, so you get yourself out.*

This way of thinking is not the way of the kingdom. The way of the kingdom is "I will take your sin, your pain, your transgressions to the cross; by my wounds you were healed" (1 Peter 2:24, my paraphrase). The way of the kingdom is light exposing the dark. The way of the kingdom is community; it is a family of faith.

Today, take an honest look at your feelings about help and where they came from. Start by asking God for help, and then don't be surprised if He nudges you to go and ask an actual person for help (even one you may have to pay). Getting help can save you years of pain.*

If you don't like asking friends for help, I get it. One thing that has enabled me to ask for help is to be a person who offers help. When my family was ill, a few friends offered to send meals. A past version of myself would have kindly declined. But the overcoming me welcomed the help. I was overwhelmed delivering room service, around the clock, to three sick kids in three separate rooms. Who knew that a Papa John's gift card could be the manifestation of kindness and care? If we are image bearers of God, then our lives should emulate the Helper. Offering help is just that: an offering. And all offerings comprise both giving and receiving. When we give, our hands are open and able to also receive.

---

* Getting help in the form of emotional support means we may be faced with truth that is hard to receive. Try to listen objectively and practice owning over offense. My mom recently gave me this gold nugget: "Offense will not only rob you of a victory, it will steal your time and lead you in the wrong direction." Remember, where there is truth, there is freedom.

CREATE SPACE

Meditate

So do not fear, for I am with you;
    do not be dismayed, for I am your God.
I will strengthen you and help you;
    I will uphold you with my righteous right hand.
    —Isaiah 41:10 NIV

Reflect

1. What is your history of help? Take a look back at your parents and grandparents to see how the way they lived has influenced your perspective.
2. What do you need help with? Who can you ask for help?
3. Who can you help?

Act

This week, take action by getting help with whatever you need help with. Then find one way to offer help.

26

SEE EVERYTHING AS A CHOICE

———

*Eyes that focus on what is beautiful bring joy to the
heart,
and hearing a good report
refreshes and strengthens the inner being.*
—Proverbs 15:30 TPT

F or years Stephen and I talked about taking a big trip for our
twentieth anniversary. We dreamed of Italy, or maybe Greece.
Somewhere in the Mediterranean where he could enjoy the beach,
I could geek out on history and architecture, and we both would
fancy the food. The timing wasn't right with our move, and, at the
time, we didn't have the finances. We both knew it wasn't in the
cards. There wasn't a need to even discuss it.

Two years later it became a possibility. There was no plan (we've never been ones to schedule things way out, as owning a business has never allowed for this) other than an unspoken promise. One March day, on a whim, Stephen said, "How about going to Holland to see the tulips? Because if not now, when?"

My great-grandparents, whom I never met, emigrated from the Netherlands to Canada. Grandma Hilda was 100 percent Dutch, yet she had never visited her family's homeland. For some reason I've always felt this strong connection to both my English and Dutch heritage. No one ever really fanned this connection; I think it's always been at the soul level. The first time I visited England, in an instant my soul felt at home. I hoped I could one day visit the Netherlands too.

My brother and sister had been lucky enough to visit the country together and loved it. My friend Christina, who spent a considerable amount of time living in Amsterdam, kept telling me I had to go. "Between the flower fields, the streets lined with gingerbread houses, and the bike bells constantly dinging like fairies fluttering by . . . this is your city, Trina; it's a fairyland."

I knew Stephen would have preferred Italy—for the food, for the sea—but he kept insisting that this would be the perfect time to see the flowers. It was a gift of kindness and consideration that I'll always treasure.

We expedited the renewal of our passports and booked our tickets in my grandma's honor.

As we made our approach into Amsterdam, I opened the rounded window blind and sighed a huge exhale for having accomplished the ride over the ocean (not my favorite pastime). Then I gasped, catching sight of the tulip fields out my window. It looked as if there were fields of rainbows, rows and rows of colors growing up and out of the ground. The beauty was astounding. The magic was already palpable.

My initial airplane reaction stuck with me the entire trip—I gasped my way through the country. Beauty was everywhere—in the city and the country, both outside and inside—the architecture boasting of canal houses that I could only assume were either inspired by fairy tales or that inspired fairy tale writers. The landscape was colored in water, windmills, and flowers as far as the eye could see. The people, tall (women effortlessly stylish and beautiful), speaking English as well as their native throaty dialect. The art, as original as it comes—van Gogh, Rembrandt, and Vermeer. The transportation, a sea of bicycles. The sound, a chorus of bike bells chiming and *jing-a-linging* in unison. The smell, stroopwafels in the city and on its outskirts the scent of hyacinth riding on the wind.

We wandered around the Herengracht, popping in and out of shops both quaint and modern. We rode bikes to the Rijksmuseum and cycled through the passage below with moody classical music booming. We traveled to Delft and witnessed how seventeenth-century pottery is still being made with the same methods. We stayed in an Airbnb in the Jordaan neighborhood and shopped at Albert Heijn for food, pretending to be locals (well that was probably just me, not Stephen). We slipped into the Keukenhof Botanical Gardens, which felt like a portal into another world, and then rode bikes through fields of tulips and hyacinths until we reached the end of the earth (so it seemed)—the North Sea. It's not often you get to live out your daydreams, tucking them in your heart and turning them into memories. But when you do, you realize it is a gift like no other.

Near the end of the trip, I checked the calendar and noticed that this was my bad week of the month (hormones at their height, which often left me depressed). In the Netherlands I was experiencing the opposite of depression. Yes, I was an ocean away from problems and worries, but I had been oceans away before and they still followed and clung to me like a stray dryer sheet. I noticed I also wasn't experiencing the many physical symptoms that I usually did in my cycle. I paid attention to this insight, this observation. Had wonder really wiped away worry? Beauty must have colored the gray away. Rest (although we walked and biked everywhere) cured my depletion and replenished my impoverished soul. Distance, as it does so well, gave me a different perspective.

I returned home on a vacation high. A day after landing, I wrapped myself in the pink coat I bought to keep warm riding through tulip fields and rode my Dutchie bike clear across busy country roads to my friend Anna-Lisa's house to deliver Gouda cheese and chocolate. Then came the crash. Jet lag hit, along with the realization that there were no gingerbread houses in my town, I couldn't ride my bike everywhere (the only fields near my house are cornfields), and my problems were waiting for me with bated breath. Relational cycles and bad habitual patterns were not broken or repaired by a wistful week away, and although a few tulips were blooming this side of the Atlantic, the weather would remain dark and dreary for some time.

The Power of Choice

While I was trying to settle back into reality, I was reminded of a walk I took in the woods a few years prior, before our move. I walked a route I rode as a kid, a way I could walk in my sleep. As I was walking, I talked with God about being overwhelmed with the crushing feeling of being stuck. I was facing several situations that needed repair, and I felt helpless.

My codependent self felt both helpless like a child and wild like an animal teeming with an inner rage that would shock those who knew me best. I wanted (needed) to do (fix) something. And yet, at the same time, I felt like a victim who could do nothing. I had never felt so trapped in all my life, with so few choices. There were so many questions that I could not answer, no matter how many scenarios I worked out in my mind. The truth was that many choices and actions were not mine to be made or taken. Just as I was beginning to learn about being interdependent, I still was dependent upon others.

"I have no choice," I mumbled under my breath.

As I rounded the corner where Bellingham becomes Wedgewood, where the mighty old oak would always greet me, I heard God's voice cut through the clutter—the clutter of everyone else's chatter, including my own, and this is what I heard: *And yet everything is a choice.*

Huh? I thought but wouldn't dare speak.

Love is a choice.

Forgiveness is a choice.

Noticing beauty is a choice.

Living in today is a choice.

Taking a shower is a choice.

Smiling is a choice.

What do you choose?

I choose life. I remembered the verse; it was there under all my clutter.

Although I couldn't see, eventually I learned that change always presents us with choice. Whether we choose change or change heaves itself upon us and makes us believe we have no choice. In actuality, all change presents us with choice, to either move forward or digress. To observe or ignore. To own or to blame. To overcome or live defeated.

At some point we all come to a dead end, a rock bottom, a closed door. A place that presents itself as having no choice. But if you'll look close enough, you'll see you're given a choice.

The choice to overcome.

A dead end is where we can turn around.
Rock bottom gives us the choice to go up.
A closed door gives the option to try another or keep knocking.

What do you choose?

Some days, months, even years, our choices seem slim to nil. But this does not mean they aren't there. I find it takes little to no effort to name the choices we don't believe we have. On the contrary, it takes both courage and creativity to name the choices, however small they may be, that we do have.

Sometimes it helps to look at the excuses. If you look close enough, you'll see a choice there too.

"I don't have a choice" is a choice.

"I can't" is a choice.

"I don't know how" is even a choice.

Have Strong Will

Together, we all have experienced our choices shrivel to levels we had not experienced prior to the pandemic and political unrest in America. If there is one thing I think we all can agree on it's that we have experienced mutual feelings of powerlessness. Sadly, many of us have found ourselves on opposing sides with some of our most beloved people—friends, parents, children, perhaps even a partner or spouse.

Those days, these times, make choice difficult. I remember a particularly hard day. It had been a big day in our country politically. I was having a hard time focusing and I felt powerless, like I know so many of you did too. On top of the pandemic and political unrest, there were those pesky hormones again, and worst of all, I was in the wake of an estranged relationship that was breaking my heart.

So I took myself to McDonald's (by now you know what this means). In feeling powerlessness, I made bad choice upon bad choice. I blurred my eyes out on social media trying to get the political pulse, when in actuality I ended up taking on the moods and opinions of everyone and their dog. I ate chocolate, lots of it. I watched the news, one pundit after the other, repeating the same fear-mongering thing. I drank too much caffeine. My subconscious concerns even played out in my dreams, down to my car falling into a body of water (worst fear ever).

The next day I felt the hangover of it all, and I felt like total garbage. In past years I would have shamed myself (which I now see was often a choice), and the shame would have led to a cycle of more small bad choices that would have accumulated into a bad day, which I would likely dramatize into a bad life.

I noticed the sun was shining (rare that time of year), so I put my face in it—even if just through the window. I then made a choice to do a few minutes of Pilates. I still felt terrible. Next choice was a shower. In the shower I talked and prayed. I asked God, *Why? Why are my feelings so big? Why do the moods of other people affect me so easily?* No answer. Only a song. An old song: "This Is the Day." In the past year I've noticed that songs I sang in church as a kid come up and out of my soul, as if they, too, were packed away in the boxes in the basement of my soul. In uncluttering we don't just uncover the junk; we uncover hidden treasures meant to help us. These songs seem to be like brooms, sweeping out the dusty corners of my mind.

This is the day that the Lord has made
I will rejoice and be glad in it.[1]

I sang the song that always sounded silly, even when I was a kid. Over and over.

"I will. I will. I will," I repeated.

"I will." I stopped and thought.

Will.

Mind. *Will.* Emotions.

Will, the auxiliary verb, means I am going to; am willing to; am determined to; am capable of.[2]

> In uncluttering we don't just uncover the junk; we uncover hidden treasures meant to help us.

Will, the noun, is defined as "the faculty of conscious and especially of deliberate action; the power of control the mind has over its own actions; the power of choosing one's own actions."[3]

Will, the verb, is "to purpose, determine on, or elect, by an act of will."[4]

Will is perhaps best defined as the power of choosing one's own actions.[5]

I cannot choose other people's actions—not the president's, not physicians', not my parents', not my partner's. I choose mine.

In these moments when I'm crowded within myself, facing what looks like no choice, when I want an answer, a break, a way out, I've learned to choose to give. I give thanks. Thank You that the sun is shining. Thank You that my children are in school. Thank You for the crimson cardinal outside my window—bright and bold among the white blanket of snow. Thank You for the warm water in my shower. Thank You for another day (even if it feels like Groundhog Day).

"Thank you" is a sacred choice. Giving thanks is the greatest form of (and the surest way to experience) autonomy.

Holocaust survivor Viktor Frankl said, "Everything can be taken from a man but one thing: the last of the human freedoms—to choose one's attitude in any given set of circumstances, to choose one's own way."[6]

Choosing your attitude, your outlook, your perspective is to choose *your* way. I often have to remind myself that a bad day, a bad month, even a bad year, does not equal a bad life—unless I choose to see it that way.

> A bad day, a bad month, even a bad year, does not equal a bad life—unless I choose to see it that way.

I don't know what choices you may be struggling to make or which you are feeling deprived of, but I do know the feeling, Dear Reader—that overwhelming pull to ignore, blame, or relent to the cycle of defeat.

Recognizing that you are living like a victim is observing.

Acknowledging that you have a choice is owning.

Deciding to make a choice, to take action—no matter how minuscule—is overcoming.

I like to think of the Netherlands as a magical land, but I know it's not. Any Dutch person would like a vacation from their country and their troubles. What I experienced was wonder, beauty, rest, and distance giving me a new perspective. And all these things can be experienced in our everyday—in ways small and large—if we will choose them.

What do you choose?

CREATE SPACE

Meditate

"I have set before you life and death, blessings and curse. Therefore choose life."

—DEUTERONOMY 30:19 ESV

Reflect

1. Where or how do you feel like you don't have choices?
2. What kind of choices are you making by not choosing?
3. Name three choices you can make this week (they can be as small as taking a shower or walk).

Act

Follow through on the choices you wrote down. Before you do them, say,

"I choose to _____."
"I choose to forgive _____."
"I choose to take a shower this morning."
"I choose to be present in this day."
"I may feel obligated to love this person, but it's my choice, and I choose love."

And then do it. Hearing yourself acknowledge choice is powerful.

27

GROW IN PEACE AND JOY

———————

There are joys which long to be ours.
—Henry Ward Beecher[1]

Uncluttering my soul has felt and looked a lot like going in circles. Round and round the same old mountain. Unpacking the same old boxes. Decluttering the same old stuff. Reframing the same old story. A little progress here and a little progress there, but not enough to show a clearing, the space, the distance, the tidy order.

There is this thing about circles: we travel in them.

In the old house I would sometimes find myself immersed in a strange living history that appeared to be repeating itself. My kids sleeping in my siblings' and my old room. Me staring out the kitchen window in a daze as I did dishes, just like my mom.

Stephen working out of the same office my dad had used. My children attending the same school and having many of the same teachers I once had. Mostly it was sweet, but sometimes when I saw the circle, I wanted to step out.

When I finally did, I found myself in the new house stuck in some of the same circles I was traveling in, in the old house. Depression, anxiety, chronic stress, grief. I suppose sometimes there are circles within circles.

I remember feeling discouraged because I was trying so hard. I was observing—finally starting to see things for what they were, and I was at the dawn of learning how to own up to my complicity. Simultaneously I was unpacking my boxes—some packed with china and others packed with behaviors and pain. I was doing the work, and I could see flecks of progress, but I wasn't sure if it counted. I still felt stuck.

One day in my reading, I went to Psalm 23 for comfort. Tucked in the tried-and-true psalm, I saw something that changed my perspective. Just after the psalmist talked of God restoring his soul (life), bringing him back to a state of health and soundness, he said, "He leads me in the paths of righteousness for His name's sake" (Psalm 23:3 AMP). Upon reading in other translations, I noticed an annotation after this portion of the text. It read that "footsteps of righteousness" can also mean "circular paths of righteousness."[2]

Circular.

I read on: "It is a common trait for sheep on the hillsides of Israel to circle their way up higher."[3]

"Circle their way"?

"They eventually form a path that keeps leading them higher. Each step we take following our Shepherd will lead us higher even though it may seem we are going in circles."[4]

Although it may feel like we are going in circles, if we follow our Shepherd, we are on a path that leads us higher. In hiking, this type of climbing is referred to as switchbacks. When it's nearly impossible to climb straight up a steep incline, switchbacks take you back and forth across the mountain until you reach the top.

During the years of my uncluttering, there have been passages in the Bible that the Lord would not let me away from: Isaiah 41, Psalm 139, Galatians 5, Psalm 91, to name a few. I'd open my Bible to read something new, and I would be led right back to where I had been. Circling around the same passages.

Growth is not always linear; it can be circular.

This was a revelation that began to speed up my transformation. Round and round, you become disoriented, believing that you are being held in the dark valleys when in actuality you are traveling through—led, and held, by Love. Round and round the mountain, it looks the same; it feels the same. Yet the altitude is changing. Round and round, you're becoming strong; your feet are becoming firmer. Round and round, your view is obstructed by the clouds. But the ominous pillows of precipitation no longer matter because, round and round, you are ascending above to panoramic views that will offer perspective on everything. Round and round, you're making your way to green pastures—wide-open spaces. Round and round, your lungs are growing robust. You are no longer holding your breath. The air is pure. Round and round, when you need a rest, there is a sheepfold safe and circular, the Shepherd on guard at the gate. Round and round, your steps are forming a path. Nor is it for you alone—it is for all those that follow behind you.

> Growth is not always linear; it can be circular.

There is this thing about circles—we can draw them.

It was an ordinary afternoon, and I was cooking an ordinary dinner (spaghetti or tacos, anyone?). To break the monotony, I popped in my AirPods and tuned in to a podcast. I have no idea whose podcast I was listening to or what the topic was. All that I recall is that the guest was author Elizabeth Gilbert, and she was telling a story about deleting all her emails. She was going through a personal crisis and concluded that she didn't need to respond to all these people, all these requests—she no longer wanted them in her space, in her circle. Delete. I thought of all the emails that were hanging at the bottom of my inbox for months. *Delete* sounded so freeing. She then began talking about drawing circles and likening them to boundaries.

My ears perked up. My boundaries were drawn with invisible ink, and they were always linear. "This is the line; you cannot cross it!" But Gilbert was talking circles. Her boundaries were not focused on who or what she kept *out*, like a wall (linear). Rather the purpose they served was to create a sacred space for who and what she wanted *in* her circle. "A boundary is a golden circle that you draw around the things that matter to you," according to Gilbert.[5]

Here I was allowing tons of junk in, while I was working on cleaning junk out. Maybe because the door is open—open to take the clutter out—it's like a welcome: "Come on in! Bring all your crap, while I'm trying to let go of mine." I'd stop my flow of letting go and let more in. I decided I needed to draw some circles of my own. I needed to clarify what is and is not allowed in my sacred space.

There is this thing about circles: we can create peace and joy within them.

Each day can feel like a circle. Dawn to dusk. Dusk to dawn. A circle that we are always tempted to step out of—into tomorrow, back to yesterday.

Yet here we are *today*.

Today is where life is lived. Today is where growth and change happen. Today is where love is given and received. Today is where we overcome.

> Today is where life is lived. Today is where growth and change happen. Today is where love is given and received. Today is where we overcome.

Today is your life.

Do you ever feel like this is practice? That you are always preparing or waiting? Or, maybe, you feel like you are just pretending—like it's some sort of movie we are all living in?

Okay, maybe that's just me and all my Enneagram Four friends because sometimes it all feels like pretending to me. But it's not. This is the real deal. The ins and outs and the boring, ordinary every day is where life is being lived; it's where joy can be found.

I used to believe that peace and joy could only be experienced when all was well and figured out and orderly. I viewed peace and joy as a prized state of mind, a trophy for those that toiled for them. Peace and joy seemed to be a destination that I was always trying to get to—to journey toward. In "today," peace and joy were always just out of reach. And I wasn't wrong about that—because I was always looking to tomorrow.

Peace and joy can only be experienced in *today*.

By some definitions joy can be described as a feeling, and it's often interchanged with happiness. But the important distinction to note is this: joy isn't dependent upon circumstances—this sets joy apart from happiness. Naturally, it's difficult to be happy when things are not going well. However, joy can be experienced in even the darkest of times. Joy isn't dependent on the goodness of our day or life. Joy is determined by the goodness of God. And the great news is that joy is not something that we wait to obtain on the other side of pain or difficulty. In fact, the joy of the Lord is our very strength (Nehemiah 8:10) in pain and difficulty.

Because joy materializes in moments, its expression is often ephemeral. Somehow, simultaneously, we experience it as tangible and fleeting. But make no mistake: there is no issue of supply and demand. Joy is ever available—even in our longing and our waiting. My greatest shift in experiencing joy came when I decided to participate in my life. Waiting, although taxing and horribly annoying, limits no one from participation. We only limit ourselves.

Remember, to participate is to come alive to our lives. And feeling alive feels a lot like joy.

Strategize for Joy

To participate, I needed a strategy. Have you ever thought of joy as a strategy? Me either, until I began to pay attention. First, I had to pay attention to my actions and results. Wishing and hoping and waiting for joy wasn't working. Second, I began to notice that individuals living a full life and experiencing joy regularly lived with intention. They didn't wake up and wait for life to happen to them; they made things happen. When someone says to them, "Have a great day," they are not the ones thinking, *I hope it's a good one.* Instead, they are the ones thinking, *I'll make it a great day.* They are strategic about life and the details therein (whom they spend time with, what they do with their time, how they trust God, their personal growth, etc.).

Strategy often implies complication or expertise. But by definition, strategy is quite simply a plan of action. Here's my formula:

Plan for joy + take action = Joy achieved

You've got what it takes to plan for joy, create space for joy, and experience joy! The following are a few strategies you can use to begin:

1. **Take the pressure off.** While I believe we can, and should, be intentional to create space for joy—ultimately joy is produced by the Holy Spirit. Joy is not a mood, feeling, or prize; joy is a fruit. The idea is not to hustle for joy; the idea (God's idea) is to yield to it (Galatians 5).

2. **Know what brings you joy.** What places, people, activities, and memories bring joy? Make a list. Include your senses. Are there particular sights, smells, or sounds that bring you joy? Think of your favorite things.

3. **Prepare for joy.** Now that you know what brings you joy, set the table. Prepare for joy like the special guest that it is. Put yourself in the way of the things that give you joy.

   If nature gives you joy—get outside. If listening to music makes you feel lighter—turn on the tunes. If the scent of roses puts you at ease, buy yourself roses. Is there anything on your list that you can schedule? Time with friends. A walk in the woods. Joy can be momentary, but we can also accommodate by planning for moments.

4. **Pay attention to joyful people.** I get it . . . some people are naturally happy and positive. They smile and laugh a lot. Hey wait, maybe there is something to that? It may come naturally to some, while you find you have to work at it; however, smiling and laughing will yield results in your life, even if you must make a practice of it. Look for patterns, behaviors, and commonalities of joyful people. Ask others why they are joyful, happy, and positive. You never know what you might learn.

   Try smiling more. I practice by smiling at myself when I pass the mirror (now I've given you something to laugh at). For so long, when I'd pass a mirror I'd catch a forlorn face looking back at me, and I finally decided I didn't like what I was seeing—I didn't like seeing myself so sad. I recently heard Mel Robbins say that she high-fives herself in the mirror every morning.[6] I love this. We have to be on our own team! And remember, repetition creates muscle memory and new neural pathways.

5. **Create.** Do things such as baking, crafting, writing, knitting, listening to music, painting, photography, or building. These are all restorative practices that will bring more peace and joy into your life. You don't have to be great at doing these things; you simply have to *enjoy* doing them. Still worried you aren't creative? Remember back to being a kid. What did you enjoy doing when it was simply for fun? Do that . . . simply for fun. Nothing makes me feel more joyful, free, and alive than swimming and riding my bike on a summer's day. As George Bernard Shaw says, "We don't stop playing because we grow old; we grow old because we stop playing."[7]

6. **Discover petite joys.** Make seemingly unenjoyable moments joyful. Listen to music that reminds you of a happy memory while you clean. Wear a colorful outfit on a dark day. If work is overwhelming, schedule a lunch break with a friend. Drink your morning coffee or tea out of your grandmother's china that you've been saving for a special occasion (every day is a special occasion). After a long day, watch a comedy before bed.

The remedy to past pain, which calls and lures like a siren, is enjoying today. Don't be tempted to step out of the circle of today, believing that joy only makes its home in distant memories or the faraway futures. Joy is at home in you *today*. The everyday is the only place where we can be, as C. S. Lewis pens it, "surprised by joy."[8]

I used to associate circles with being stuck; now I find them synonymous with stride. Our progress might not boast of a quick climb or sudden success, but one that, in time, shows a well-worn path of transformation. In my circles I've had to learn that growth isn't necessarily measured by how our situation has changed; it's measured best by how we respond to the situation. Heart and soul transformation can never be fully measured by humans.

> Growth isn't necessarily measured by how our situation has changed; it's measured best by how we respond to the situation.

As you work to unclutter your soul, be aware that some people will not notice the change taking place in you. They will not see the change within your circles. Keep climbing. Growth can be hard to measure. Especially when we live up close to people. Especially if others haven't experienced the same type of growth in their life. Especially when the growth is happening deep inside of you. Some people are situation and surface focused. Don't worry about them—you're too busy doing the heart work anyway.

CREATE SPACE

Meditate

For you shall go out in joy
    and be led forth in peace;
the mountains and the hills before you
    shall break forth into singing,
    and all the trees of the field shall clap their
        hands.
    —Isaiah 55:12 ESV

Reflect

1. Do you feel like you are going in circles? What have you been circling around?
2. Do you need to draw a sacred circle? What do you need to draw it around?
3. Do you tend to look back or always long for what's ahead? What brings you joy?

Act

Create your own strategies for joy. Plan for and schedule joy into your calendar this week. *Bonus:* start smiling and high-fiving yourself in the mirror.

A BLOOM IS FIRST A BUD

*All of us have had the experience of a sudden
joy that came when nothing in the world had
forewarned us of its coming—a joy so thrilling that
if it was born of misery we remembered even the
misery with tenderness.*

—Antoine de Saint-Exupéry[1]

At this point in our journey, Dear Reader, I imagine us taking a break. We've been on a long, winding journey. With stops and goes. Unpacking and sorting. Steps and circles. Mystery and clarity. Letting go and owning. If our visit were in person, I'd put the kettle on and we'd pause from our uncluttering. With a mug of steaming tea warming our hands, I'd ask about your journey inward—about the design of *your* soul. And then I'd share in more detail about mine. I imagine we would be astonished at how different, yet similar, our journeys have been. We'd marvel at the progress, and we would observe the space we've created. We'd high-five each other like teammates do at the end of a game.

Although this is not the end.

I should like to tell you that this work is one and done, and that when you remove the clutter—whether mental, emotional, spiritual, physical—it is gone for good. But you don't need me to tell you that this is not the case. You know this already. You know the elixir of feeling free—a day in which nothing or no one has a hold on you. And you know the plunge of disappointment that can surface the very next day, waking up to a familiar weight as you peer through the window of your soul into a soupy fog.

You are no stranger to the cycle of it all, are you? So why do this work at all? And will this work ever be done? Because it can feel defeating. The highs and lows. Certainty and confusion. Clean and cluttered. Clouds and clear skies. *Can't my soul make up its mind?*

Weary traveler, this is exactly what the soul—our mind, will, and emotions—must do: make up its mind, engage its will, know its emotions. Our souls must decide—again and again—observe, own, and overcome.

As you're experiencing, tending your soul takes hard work coupled with the surrender of yielding. An ebb and flow. A give and take. With all this work, you aren't just earning a clearer mind, you're also building mental muscle and emotional fortitude. Observing, owning, and overcoming isn't just a long-form process; it's a tool that you can put into practice in your everyday.

Our high five, then, is to cheer one another on. To say, "Don't give up. Keep going. You're not alone—I'm on your team!"

Life is not paradoxically good or bad. A good life will have bad days. And a hard life will not be devoid of good. Life will still present setbacks and disappointments, but you now have tools and fortitude to weather what comes your way—you have courage in adversity.

When I landed in my temporary home, spring was approaching. On the calendar, in my heart, on the street sign. It was evident that this was a new season all around. With a most potent mix of leftover fears and fresh hope, I convinced myself that I was ready for change. I just hadn't understood that the biggest change taking place would be *in me.* As the adrenaline waned, as I became discouraged to find myself dealing with old clutter at a new address, as I discovered that hard choices and obedience were not akin to the sprinkling of pixie dust, I heard the voice of Love say to me, *Don't mistake a bud for a bloom.*

Spring, I had forgotten, was not all greens and pinks. Sun and blooms.

Spring is first seeds and dirt. Dark and damp.

And where I'm from, spring at first looks and feels a lot like winter. Sometimes it still snows. Nothing looks or feels like spring. But the underground knows different. The seed is stretching in the dark. Change is slow and secret, a private business between Creator and creation.

I began to ponder how the work of change is often overlooked and never celebrated until . . . the bloom. In an instant it appears as if seasons change and the flowers burst into color. But we know better. We understand the time and the toil. We have concluded that we *can* create space in the tight places. And now we can choose to celebrate the bud as much as the bloom. There is space for peace and joy *today* if we choose it.

It is spring, again, and change is in the air again. I can smell it, sweet like the hyacinth fields in Holland. It's been three years of intense observing, owning, and overcoming—of decorating my heart and soul. Years and years of this little bud pushing to bloom. So many stops, so many steps, battling, waiting, obeying, and staying—now it is time for us to go.

> There is space for peace and joy *today* if we choose it.

As I finish this book, we are preparing

to move to that place that we often drove through, to a town whose name will never let me forget all my springs. I'm looking forward to decorating a lived-in home once again. A home I can describe only as the four walls of God's kindness. As we pack our belongings into boxes, I'll continue the unpacking and uncluttering of my soul, always remembering that the blessing and the wide-open space isn't an arrival; it is a place accessed through obedience and the presence of God. We must stop our search for the perfect life and turn our gaze to the Perfect One.

Life is unsure and uncertain. Jesus told us that it's a sure thing that we'd have trouble in this world. *But* He then followed with "*take heart!* I have overcome the world."[2] All of our troubles and uncertainties are temporary. Let's be sure of this: for as many times as we journey inward, sorting through our soul clutter, goodness and unfailing love will be pursuing us all the days of our lives.[3] As surely as the sun will rise, He will appear.[4] The lovers of God may suffer adversity and stumble seven times, but they will continue to rise over and over again.[5]

> We must stop our search for the perfect life and turn our gaze to the Perfect One.

Whatever comes your way, you will make it through. And should you look back at your journey, the crowded, dilapidated dwelling that was once your home will look nothing like the spacious residence of your soul. You'll know the clutter by its name, you'll recognize what was once pain, you'll tell the story of the path you traveled, helping others along their way, and, as you do, you'll find the floor plan of your soul broadened and colored in hues of goodness and unfailing love.

Download Trina's Uncluttering Celebratory playlist at
trinamcneilly.com/celebrateplaylist

ACKNOWLEDGMENTS

Writing comes naturally to me; however, organizing my thoughts, stories, and research for this book proved arduous. This book began during a tumultuous time in my personal life, took shape, and was written during a global pandemic, then was edited during an out-of-state move (this all gave me ample opportunity to continue the work of uncluttering both my soul and home). Many times I came close to relinquishing this project and keeping these words tucked in the privacy of my personal journals. But for God; but for you, Dear Reader; but for the following beloved people that cheered me on, believed in me, and tangibly helped me, I would not have made it through.

Many thanks to my agent, Angela Scheff, who talked through this concept with me for years, helps me to think well about decisions, and is a wonderful advocate. I'm lucky to have you on my team.

Thank you to Debbie Wickwire, my editor, for your excitement around this concept, your constant encouragement and email prayers, and your ability to see what I couldn't. You are a gem.

Thanks also to Jennifer McNeil for your editorial work, advocating for the reader, and offering me cosy-crime recommendations.

Acknowledgments

Thank you also to the entire team at W. You've brought expertise and excellence to this work and have made me feel like I'm part of a team.

Thank you to my readers. Choosing a book is choosing to keep company with another. I'm honored that you would choose my words (in books or online). My prayer is that my writing opens a door to hope and healing, provides fresh insight, and stirs your imagination.

Many thanks to Abby Lesburg, my heaven-sent intern. There is no way I could have written a book and started a podcast without your help and input. Thanks for being on Team La La Lovely.

Much gratitude to Mastermind Group, who has continually encouraged me and offered wise insight and advice: Niki Hardy, Adriel Booker, Kathy Izard, Rachel Awtrey, Kara-Kae James. Thank you also to my friend and fellow author Nicole Zasowski, who cheers me on and keeps me company as we've traveled through the publishing process together.

Thank you dearly to friends and family who have talked through this concept, read through this book at various stages, and helped me remember the past: Cindy Tompkins, Amy Tompkins, Pat VanTil, Jeremy DeWeeredt, Christina Bacino, Rebekah Lyons, Anna-Lisa Horton, Erin Campbell, Abby Lesburg.

Much love and many thanks to girlfriends who color my gray days with laughter, are the loveliest characters in my stories, and who always lend an ear and hold me up when I'm overwhelmed: Rebekah Lyons, Jen DeWeeredt, Kim Gilbertson, Anna-Lisa Horton, Maggie Sullivan, Jenny Ostrowski, Erin Campbell, Christina Bacino, Lindsay Tompkins, Shea McNeilly, Angela Nowery, Lori Eickoff, Liz Willard, Lisa Seaton, Leah Gregory.

To my friend Kendell Larson, who has stepped into the overwhelm of my life and been a helper. Helping me with my kiddies

(#CampKendell forever), ensuring stuffed animals don't take over our home, and helping us through two very emotional moves.

Much love and gratitude to my prayer warriors who are wise, steadfast, and so kind: Memaw McNeilly; my wonderful in-laws Dave and Martha McNeilly; my adopted grandparents, Roy and Evelyn Gipson; and Gloria Geraldo, who sent me encouraging words at just the right time.

Amy and J.J., we've been writing stories together our whole lives (and now show notes). I'm so grateful we have one another as keepers of a collective family story. I treasure our tales of old (even the hard ones), but I am excited about the new stories God is authoring with our lives. Amy, thank you for being our dreamer, seeing things before we can. Thank you for never boring of talking through ideas and concepts and for holding the vision when I seem to lose it.

Dad, you have taught me to be a strong person. I've learned invaluable lessons from you. Your methods, idioms, stories, and wisdom continue to guide me. Thank you for teaching me how to be a generous person and live a generous life. When I see your little orations of books, objects of meaning, and notes peppered throughout your house, it makes me happy to see the history behind my methodology. Thank you for giving me a love for words and print.

Mom, you have given me the precious gift of unconditional love and acceptance. Thank you for taking all my calls (even in the middle of the night) and verbally processing everything with me. You always have the right words at the right time, a result of spending so much time in God's Word. Thank you for never judging my worries and always gently leading me back to truth, peace, and the power of the cross. You are so strong, "steel wrapped in velvet" as Pastor Mayo used to say. I hope I can grow into being the kind of mom and Gommy that you are (everyone's favorite!).

Acknowledgments

To my darling children who I learn from every day: Ella, your passion and boldness astounds and challenges me. Thank you for helping me grow; you are precious to me. Luke, your discipline and commitment is rare and inspires me to be better. Thank you for smiles, hugs, and teenage humor. Liam, your empathy and ability to comprehend and conversate never ceases to amaze and comfort me. Thank you for caring for me. Rocco, your tender heart toward God and people is quite special. Your passion to pray for others is beautiful. Thank you for always praying for me (and making me laugh) when I get overwhelmed. Jai, you make our family complete. Your heart to keep close and celebrate those you love is a beautiful thing. Thank you for teaching me how to show up, better, for those that I love. I'm proud of you.

Stephen, thank you for being my teammate, for giving me a beautiful place to write, and for being an amazing dad. You always push me toward growth and change, keeping me on the edge of my seat. Your influence has helped me to see what I often miss and unclutter the hidden parts of my heart and my soul—thank you for patience and loyalty. We've weathered rough seas and become both stronger and softer because of it. I love you, always.

All thanks, glory, and honor to God. Thank you, God, for fathering me, Jesus for never leaving me, and the Holy Spirit for shining the torchlight into the cellar of my soul. I cannot imagine where I would be were it not for the unconditional love and ever-present help of God. Thank you, once again, for giving me words and allowing me to pour out into this sacred story (Psalm 45:1).

NOTES

The Interior Design of Our Lives
1. Paraphrase from Marcel Proust, *Remembrance of Things Past*, vol. 5: *The Prisoner*, trans. C. K. Scott Moncrieff (London: Penguin Classics, 2016), http://gutenberg.net.au/ebooks03/0300501.txt.

Part 1: Observe
1. John O'Donohue, *Beauty: The Invisible Embrace; Rediscovering the True Sources of Compassion, Serenity, and Hope* (New York, HarperCollins Perennial, 2005), 39.

Chapter 1: Listen to the Soundtrack of Your Soul
1. C. Sreechinth, *Musings of Carl Jung* (Roosevelt, UT: UB Tech, 2018), 41.
2. "Depression," World Health Organization, January 30, 2020, https://www.who.int/news-room/fact-sheets/detail/depression.
3. "Facts & Statistics," Anxiety and Depression Association of America, last updated April 21, 2021, https://adaa.org/understanding-anxiety/facts-statistics.
4. *Key Substance Use and Mental Health Indicators in the United States: Results from the 2018 National Survey on Drug Use and Health* (Rockville, MD: SAMHSA, 2019), 2, https://www.samhsa.gov/data/sites/default/files/cbhsq-reports/NSDUHNationalFindingsReport2018/NSDUHNationalFindingsReport2018.pdf.
5. Ephesians 3:17.
6. 1 Corinthians 3:16.
7. Craig von Buseck, "What Are the Three Parts of Man?," CBN, accessed June 26, 2021, https://www1.cbn.com/questions/what-are-the-three-parts-of-man.

Chapter 2: Accept a Custom Plan
1. Quote by Brittany Burgunder: "Sometimes the process . . . ," Goodreads, accessed July 4, 2021, https://www.goodreads.com/quotes/9386260-sometimes-the-process-of-growth-looks-a-lot-like-destruction.
2. James 2:17.

3. Megan Rossi, "Forget Five-a-day!" DailyMail.com, last updated October 16, 2019, https://www.dailymail.co.uk/femail/article-7568849/Are-getting-30-week.html.

Chapter 3: Inventory Your Clutter

1. Viktor Frankl, *Man's Search for Meaning* (Boston, MA: Beach Press, 2006), 112.
2. David A. Seamands, *Healing for Damaged Emotions* (Colorado Springs: David C. Cook, 2015).
3. *Merriam-Webster.com Dictionary*, s.v. "fear," accessed June 27, 2021, https://www.merriam-webster.com/dictionary/fear.
4. Joyce Meyer, *Battlefield of the Mind: Winning the Battle in Your Mind* (New York: Warner Faith: 1995), 108.
5. *Merriam-Webster.com Dictionary*, s.v. "worry," accessed June 26, 2021, https://www.merriam-webster.com/dictionary/worry.
6. *Merriam-Webster.com Dictionary*, s.v. "anticipate," accessed June 26, 2021, https://www.merriam-webster.com/dictionary/anticipate.
7. Kimberly Holland, "Everything You Need to Know About Anxiety," Healthline, last updated September 3, 2020, https://www.healthline.com/health/anxiety.
8. Dr. Rangan Chatterjee, "What Exactly Is Anxiety?," interview on *BBC Breakfast*, Facebook video, 3:07, April 6, 2020, https://www.facebook.com/watch/?v=2730499217027784.
9. "Stress Management: Know Your Triggers," Mayo Clinic, March 28, 2019, https://www.mayoclinic.org/healthy-lifestyle/stress-management/in-depth/stress-management/art-20044151.
10. Frank Drummond, "Stress: The 'Health Epidemic of the 21st Century,'" *HCA Healthcare Today*, April 30, 2019, https://hcatodayblog.com/2019/04/30/stress-the-health-epidemic-of-the-21st-century/.
11. Mithu Storoni, *Stress Proof: The Scientific Solution to Protect Your Brain and Body—And Be More Resilient Every Day* (New York: TarcherPerigee, 2017), 9.
12. Elyssa Barbash, "Different Types of Trauma: Small 't' versus Large 'T,'" *Psychology Today*, March 13, 2017, https://www.psychologytoday.com/us/blog/trauma-and-hope/201703/different-types-trauma-small-t-versus-large-t.
13. Barbash, "Different Types of Trauma."
14. "Depression," World Health Organization, January 30, 2020, https://www.who.int/news-room/fact-sheets/detail/depression.
15. "Melancholy Is the Pleasure of Being Sad," Quote Investigator, January 29, 2015, https://quoteinvestigator.com/2015/01/29/melancholy/.
16. Guy Winch, "The Important Difference Between Sadness and Depression," *Psychology Today*, October 2, 2015, https://www.psychologytoday.com/us/blog/the-squeaky-wheel/201510/the-important-difference-between-sadness-and-depression.
17. Brené Brown, *Daring Greatly: How the Courage to Be Vulnerable Transforms the Way We Live, Parent, and Lead* (New York: Avery, 2013), 69.
18. Lindsay Dodgson, "A Psychotherapist Says That There Are Four Types of Shame: Here's What They Are and How They Affect Us," *Independent*, April 4, 2018, https://www.independent.co.uk/life-style/health-and-families/healthy-living/different-types-shame-psychology-a8287981.html.
19. Kirsten Weir, "Forgiveness Can Improve Mental and Physical Health," *Monitor*

on Psychology 48, no. 1 (January 2017): 30, American Psychological Association, https://www.apa.org/monitor/2017/01/ce-corner/.

Chapter 4: Pay Attention to Your Body

1. Ann Patchett, *State of Wonder* (London: A&C Black, 2011), 246.

Chapter 5: Know Your (Emotional) Age

1. Quote by Maya Angelou: "If you happen to be white . . . ," Goodreads, accessed on July 4, 2021, https://www.goodreads.com/quotes/1226838-if-you-happen-to-be -white-in-a-white-country.
2. Christine Langley-Obaugh, quoted in Stark Raving, "We Repeat the Things We Do Not Repair," Medium, April 2, 2019, https://medium.com/invisible-illness /we-repeat-the-things-we-do-not-repair-76ab29153208.

Chapter 6: Say Goodbye to Comfy Clutter

1. Gaston Bachelard, *The Poetics of Space: The Classical Look at How We Experience Places* (New York: Penguin, 2014), 28.
2. Quote by Tony Robbins: "Change happens . . . ," Goodreads, accessed June 26, 2021, https://www.goodreads.com/quotes/642741-change-happens-when-the-pain-of -staying-the-same-is.

Chapter 7: Don't Forget the Boxes in the Basement

1 Juwen Perrow, "The Gift of a Box Full of Darkness," *New York Times*, May 24, 2018, https://www.nytimes.com/2018/05/24/well/gifts-gratitude-friendship-loss-grief -stress-poetry.html.
2. Max Lucado, "Strongholds," Max Lucado: Words of Hope and Help (website), September 2015, https://maxlucado.com/strongholds/.
3. *Cambridge Advanced Learner's Dictionary and Thesaurus*, s.v. "stronghold," https:// dictionary.cambridge.org/us/dictionary/english/stronghold.
4. Joyce Meyer, "Satan's Strongholds," Joyce Meyer Ministries, March 6, 2020, https://joycemeyer.org/en/dailydevo/2020/03/0306-Satans-Strongholds.
5. Caroline Leaf, "You Are Not a Victim of Your Biology!," *Dr. Leaf* (blog), October 3, 2018, https://drleaf.com/blogs/news/you-are-not-a-victim-of-your-biology.
6. Mary Kassian, "Run into the Stronghold (Psa 9:9–10)," Fighter Verses, July 27, 2014, https://fighterverses.com/blog-post/run-into-the-stronghold-psa-99-10/.
7. Kassian, "Run into the Stronghold."

Chapter 8: Go Through to Get Out

1. Parker J. Palmer, *Let Your Life Speak: Listening for the Voice of Vocation* (San Francisco: Jossey-Bass, 2000), 85.
2. Helen Oxenbury and Michael Rosen, *We're Going on a Bear Hunt* (New York: Little Simon, 1997).
3. Jon Kabat-Zinn, *Wherever You Go, There You Are: Mindfulness Meditation in Everyday Life* (1994; repr., New York: Hachette Books, 2005), xiii.

Notes

Chapter 9: Participate in Your Life

1. Toni Bernhard, "Who Didn't Say That? Ten Surprising Misattributed Quotations," *Psychology Today*, July 11, 2013, https://www.psychologytoday.com/us/blog /turning-straw-gold/201307/who-didn-t-say-ten-surprising-misattributed-quotations.
2. John O'Donohue, *Beauty: The Invisible Embrace; Rediscovering the True Sources of Compassion, Serenity, and Hope* (New York: HarperCollins Perennial, 2005), 42.

Chapter 10: Imagine Space

1. George MacDonald, "The Imagination: Its Functions and Its Culture," in *The Imagination: And Other Essays* (Boston, MA: D. Lothrop and Company, 1883), 28.
2. Concept from Gaston Bachelard, *The Poetics of Space: The Classical Look at How We Experience Intimate Spaces* (Boston, MA: Beacon Press, 1969).
3. C. S. Lewis, *Mere Christianity* (1952; repr., New York: HarperOne, 2001), 205.
4. Matthew 9:17.

Part 2: Own

1. Brené Brown, *The Gifts of Imperfection: Let Go of Who You Think You're Supposed to Be and Embrace Who You Are* (Center City, MN: Hazelden Publishing, 2010), ix.

Chapter 11: Tell Yourself the Truth

1. "Nora Ephron, '62 Addressed the Graduates of 1996," Wellesley College, accessed July 4, 2021, https://www.wellesley.edu/events/commencement/archives /1996commencement.
2. Myquillyn Smith (@thenester), "Admire it without needing to acquire it," Instagram, June 5, 2019, https://www.instagram.com/p/ByVFveYgn1K.
3. *Cambridge Advanced Learner's Dictionary and Thesaurus*, s.v. "own-up," https:// dictionary.cambridge.org/us/dictionary/english/own-up.

Chapter 12: Embrace Mystery

1. Frank Herbert, *Dune* (New York: Penguin, 2019), 38.
2. David Barnett, "Agatha Christie: Why We Still Love Her 'Cosy Crime' Mysteries," *Independent*, September 14, 2017, https://www.independent.co.uk/news/long_reads /agatha-christie-cosy-crime-novels-murder-mystery-writer-why-we-love-a7942901.html.

Chapter 13: Be a Thought Leader

1. James Allen, *Above Life's Turmoil* (London: L. N. Fowler, 1910), 82, https://archive .org/details/in.ernet.dli.2015.94028/page/n81/.
2. Alex Soojung-Kim Pang, *Rest: Why You Get More Done When You Work Less* (New York: Basic Books, 2018), 93.

Chapter 14: Declare Your Decisions

1. John C. Maxwell, Facebook, November 30, 2020, https://www.facebook.com/ watch/?v=10158801336637954.

2. Sheryl Sandberg, *Lean In: Women, Work, and the Will to Lead* (New York: Knopf, 2013), 129.

3. Amanda Steinberg, *Worth It: Your Life, Your Money, Your Terms* (New York: Gallery Books, 2017), 110.

4. James Clear, *Atomic Habits: An Easy & Proven Way to Build Good Habits & Break Bad Ones* (New York: Avery, 2018), 142.

Chapter 15: Design New Patterns

1. Julia Cameron, "Clearing a Path: The Magic of Decluttering," The Artist's Way, February 7, 2017, https://juliacameronlive.com/2017/02/07/clearing-a-path-the-magic-of-decluttering.

2. Strest: The Stress Reduction Spot (website), accessed June 26, 2021, https://strestllc.com/.

Chapter 16: Confess Your Expectations

1. Paul Scanlon (@PaulScanlonUK), "If you don't manage your expectations, you will have to manage your disappointments. #managexpectations," Facebook, video, 1:55, December 21, 2019, https://www.facebook.com/watch/?v=606202910126719.

Chapter 17: Talk About the Things You Can't Talk About

1. George Bernard Shaw, *Immaturity* (London: Constable and Company 1931), xlv.

2. Natalie Baker, "We Are Only As Sick As Our Secrets," American Addiction Centers, last updated January 30, 2017, https://www.recovery.org/were-only-as-sick-as-our-secrets/.

3. Pauline Boss, "Navigating Loss Without Closure," July 16, 2020, in *On Being*, produced by Krista Tippett, podcast, MP3 audio, 50:53, https://onbeing.org/programs/pauline-boss-navigating-loss-without-closure/.

4. "Shiva (Judaism)," Wikipedia, last updated June 16, 2021, https://en.wikipedia.org/wiki/Shiva_(Judaism).

Chapter 18: Be at Home with Yourself

1. Quote by Mark Twain: "The worst loneliness is . . . ," Goodreads, accessed August 20, 2021, https://www.goodreads.com/quotes/83918-the-worst-loneliness-is-to-not-be-comfortable-with-yourself.

Chapter 19: Tell Yourself a New Story

1. Marcus Aurelius, quoted in Mithu Storoni, *Stress Proof: The Scientific Solution to Protect Your Brain and Body—and Be More Resilient Every Day* (New York: TarcherPerigee, 2017), 26.

2. Esther Perel, "Relationships and How They Shape Us," *Feel Better, Live More*, produced by Rangan Chatterjee, podcast, YouTube video, 1:15:54, June 30, 2020, https://www.youtube.com/watch?v=_Yaka0RHYfo.

3. Perel, "Relationships and How They Shape Us."

4. *Merriam-Webster.com Dictionary*, s.v. "overcome," accessed June 26, 2021, https://www.merriam-webster.com/dictionary/overcome.

Chapter 20: Take Your Power Back

1. Joyce Meyer, *Battlefield of the Mind: Winning the Battle in Your Mind* (New York: Warner Faith, 1995), 231.
2. Danny Silk, *Keep Your Love On: Connection, Communication & Boundaries* (New York: Loving On Purpose, 2013), 26.
3. Silk, *Keep Your Love On*, 26.
4. Melody Beattie, "Owning Our Power," Melody Beattie (website), July 6, 2020, https://melodybeattie.com/owning-our-power/.
5. Melody Beattie, "Owning Our Power," Melody Beattie (website), August 27, 2020, https://melodybeattie.com/owning-power-2/.

Chapter 21: Trust God with Your Time

1. Madeleine L'Engle, *An Acceptable Time* (New York: Macmillan, 2007), 96.
2. *The American Heritage Dictionary of the English Language*, s.v. "slump," (New York: Houghton Mifflin, 2016).

Chapter 22: Pursue Peace

1. Hans Hofmann, quoted in Rachel Ashwell, *Shabby Chic Interiors: My Rooms, Treasures, and Trinkets* (New York: CICO Books, 2018), 116.
2. Emily P. Freeman, *The Next Right Thing: A Simple, Soulful Practice for Making Right Decisions* (Grand Rapids: Revell, 2019), 27.

Chapter 23: Engage to Find a Better Way

1. John O'Donohue, *Beauty: The Invisible Embrace; Rediscovering the True Sources of Compassion, Serenity, and Hope* (New York: HarperCollins Perennial, 2005), 56.
2. "Strong's Greek: 3340. metanoeó," accessed June 26, 2021, BibleHub, https://biblehub.com/greek/3340.htm.
3. Lexico.com, s.v. "equanimity," accessed August 20, 2021, https://www.lexico.com/en/definition/equanimity.
4. Mithu Storoni, *Stress Proof: The Scientific Solution to Protect Your Brain and Body—and Be More Resilient Every Day* (New York: TarcherPerigee, 2017), 19.
5. Storoni, *Stress Proof*, 25.
6. Storoni, 25–26, emphasis mine.
7. Storoni, 51.
8. Storoni, 26.

Chapter 24: Nurture and Nourish

1. Quote by Socrates: "My friend . . . ," Goodreads, accessed June 26, 2021, https://www.goodreads.com/quotes/398845-my-friend-care-for-your-psyche-know-thyself-for-once-we-know.

2. Alice Fleerackers, "The Simple Dutch Cure for Stress," Nautilus, November 8, 2019, https://nautil.us/blog/the-simple-dutch-cure-for-stress.

3. Maddy Savage, "Friluftsliv: The Nordic Concept of Getting Outdoors," BBC, December 10, 2017, https://www.bbc.com/worklife/article/20171211-friluftsliv -the-nordic-concept-of-getting-outdoors.

4. Michele Debczak, "Uitwaaien, or Outblowing, Is the Dutch Cure for the Winter Blues," Mental Floss, November 12, 2019, https://www.mentalfloss.com/article /607707/uitwaaien-outblowing-dutch-cure%20for-winter-blues.

5. Eva Selhub, "Nutritional Psychiatry: Your Brain on Food," Harvard Health Publishing, March 26, 2020, https://www.health.harvard.edu/blog/nutritional -psychiatry-your-brain-on-food-201511168626.

6. Daniel Amen, "8 Mood Foods That Fight Depression," Amen Clinics, December 30, 2019, https://www.amenclinics.com/blog/8-mood-foods-that-fight -depression/.

7. Amen, "8 Mood Foods That Fight Depression."

8. 1 Kings 18–19.

Chapter 25: Ask for Help

1. Charlie Mackesy, *The Boy, the Mole, the Fox and the Horse* (New York: HarperOne, 2019), no page number.

2. John C. Maxwell, *Running with Giants: What Old Testament Heroes Want You to Know About Life and Leadership* (New York: Warner Books, 2002), 83.

Chapter 26: See Everything as a Choice

1. Dr. Hawn, "History of Hymns: 'This Is the Day,'" United Methodist Church Discipleship Ministries, June 12, 2013, https://www.umcdiscipleship.org /resources/history-of-hymns-this-is-the-day.

2. *Dictionary.com Unabridged*, s.v. "will," accessed July 5, 2021, https://www .dictionary.com/browse/will.

3. *Dictionary.com Unabridged*, s.v. "will."

4. *Dictionary.com Unabridged*, s.v. "will."

5. *Dictionary.com Unabridged*, s.v. "will."

6. Viktor E. Frankl, *Man's Search for Meaning* (Boston, MA: Beach Press, 2006), 66.

Chapter 27: Grow in Peace and Joy

1. Henry Ward Beecher, *Life Thoughts: Gathered from the Extemporaneous Discourses of Henry Ward Beecher* (Boston: Phillips, Sampson and Co., 1859), 103.

2. Brian Simmons, *The Passion Translation: The New Testament with Psalms, Proverbs, and Song of Songs* (Savage, MN: BroadStreet, 2020), Psalm 23:3nf.

3. Simmons, *Passion Translation*, Psalm 23:3nf.

4. Simmons, Psalm 23:3nf.

5. Debra Wallace, "Author Elizabeth Gilbert Shares Her Three Most Empowering Words for an Effective and Happy Life: 'I Don't Care!,'" *Parade*, October 7, 2019, https://parade.com/932863/debrawallace/author-elizabeth-gilbert-shares-her-three -most-empowering-words-for-an-effective-and-happy-life-i-dont-care/.

Notes

6. Mel Robbins (@melrobbins), "I have a simple rule that will change your life: Never leave a bathroom without high-fiving the person you see in the mirror. It's a simple and shockingly . . ." Twitter, November 14, 2020, 12:29 p.m., https://twitter.com /melrobbins/status/1327679946970570756?lang=en.
7. Quote by George Bernard Shaw: "We don't stop playing . . . ," Goodreads, accessed July 5, 2021, https://www.goodreads.com/quotes/413462-we-don-t-stop-playing -because-we-grow-old-we-grow.
8. C. S. Lewis, *Surprised by Joy: The Shape of My Early Life* (1955; repr., New York: HarperOne, 2017).

A Bloom Is First a Bud

1. Quote by Antoine de Saint-Exupéry: "I had thought myself lost . . . ," Goodreads, accessed July 5, 2021, https://www.goodreads.com/quotes/6681791-i-had-thought -myself-lost-had-touched-the-very-bottom.
2. John 16:33 NIV, emphasis mine.
3. Psalm 23:6.
4. Hosea 6:3.
5. Proverbs 24:16.

ABOUT THE AUTHOR

Trina McNeilly is the author and founder of La La Lovely, where she has been writing and building community online for thirteen years, sharing matters of the heart and design-related finds. With an eye for beauty, Trina finds inspiration in styled spaces, broken places, and everywhere in between. In 2018 she authored *La La Lovely: The Art of Finding Beauty in the Everyday*. Through her soulful writing and *The Lovely Life* podcast, Trina is the voice of a trusted friend, helping others navigate their inner life and find peace and joy in their everyday lives, no matter what they are going through. Her work has been featured in the *New York Times* and *Life:Beautiful* and on Apartment Therapy. Trina resides in Nashville, Tennessee, with her husband and their four children.

Connect with Trina at trinamcneilly.com
Instagram @trina_mcneilly
Facebook @trinamcneillyauthor

If you've been inspired by *Unclutter Your Soul*, I'd love to offer you further encouragement and resources to help you continue your journey in creating space in your everyday life for more peace and joy.

Visit **trinamcneilly.com**
for Free Resources and Downloads

- The Lovely Life Podcast
- Information on My Other Publications
- Blog Posts
- Encouragement and Inspiration

Let's continue to overcome overwhelm together!

Trina